PUBLIC SPEAKING

Public Speaking Guide to Manage Shyness, Stop Anxiety and Unlock Leadership Skills

(The Ultimate Handbook for Mastering Effective Communication)

John Morgan

Published by Rob Miles

© John Morgan

All Rights Reserved

Conversation Skills: Public Speaking Guide to Manage Shyness, Stop Anxiety and Unlock Leadership Skills (The Ultimate Handbook for Mastering Effective Communication)

ISBN 978-1-989990-18-6

All rights reserved. No part of this guide may be reproduced in any form without permission in writing from the publisher except in the case of brief quotations embodied in critical articles or reviews.

Legal & Disclaimer

The information contained in this book is not designed to replace or take the place of any form of medicine or professional medical advice. The information in this book has been provided for educational and entertainment purposes only.

The information contained in this book has been compiled from sources deemed reliable, and it is accurate to the best of the Author's knowledge; however, the Author cannot guarantee its accuracy and validity and cannot be held liable for any errors or omissions. Changes are periodically made to this book. You must consult your doctor or get professional medical advice before using any of the suggested remedies, techniques, or information in this book.

Upon using the information contained in this book, you agree to hold harmless the Author from and against any damages, costs, and expenses, including any legal fees potentially resulting from the application of any of the information provided by this guide. This disclaimer applies to any damages or injury caused by the use and application, whether directly or indirectly, of any advice or information presented, whether for breach of contract, tort, negligence, personal injury, criminal intent, or under any other cause of action.

You agree to accept all risks of using the information presented inside this book. You need to consult a professional medical practitioner in order to ensure you are both able and healthy enough to participate in this program.

Table of Contents

INTRODUCTION 1

CHAPTER 1: ASSUMING A DANCING POSITION 5

CHAPTER 2: IMPORTANCE OF PUBLIC SPEAKING 21

CHAPTER 3: HOW TO USE EYE CONTACT 26

CHAPTER 4: HOW TO BEAT YOUR GLOSSOPHOBIA 31

CHAPTER 5: PRACTICING CORRECTLY 44

CHAPTER 6: SYMPTOMS ARISING FROM FEAR OF PUBLIC SPEAKING 51

CHAPTER 7: BEGIN TO REDUCE THE FEAR OR ELIMINATE IT COMPLETELY 57

CHAPTER 8: STRATEGIES AND TECHNIQUES YOU CAN USE 65

CHAPTER 9: PUBLIC SPEAKING IS EASY YOUR BODY WILL HELP! 74

CHAPTER 10: MEMORY 84

CHAPTER 11: PERFECTION: THE GREAT ENEMY 92

CHAPTER 12: LET'S BREATHE 95

CHAPTER 13: EVERYONE CAN BE A GOOD SPEAKER 102

CHAPTER 14: UNDERSTANDING YOUR AUDIENCE 111

CHAPTER 15: PRELIMINARY CONSIDERATIONS FOR YOUR SPEECH 118

CHAPTER 16: THE BODY 121

CHAPTER 17: THE HOW 130

CHAPTER 18: PEAK PERFORMANCE TIPS 141

CHAPTER 19: PRE-PREPARATION 148

CHAPTER 20: PUBLIC SPEAKING VISUALIZATION 160

CHAPTER 21: HAVE A CLEAR FOCUS / MESSAGE 165

CHAPTER 22: REALISM NOT PERFECTION 178

CHAPTER 23: GETTING YOUR MESSAGE ACROSS 183

CONCLUSION 190

Introduction

Words are pretty amazing. For something that can't be manipulated physically, it brings a considerable amount of impact to people. And more often than not, this impact is not limited to a single person.

Communication is rarely a one-sided affair. The said case can only happen in two circumstances. First is when an individual undergoes the process of intrapersonal communication which is vital for personal growth. In this process, an individual can freely confront his fears, thoughts and dreams among other things that he may have kept hidden from the rest of the world. Communication only takes place only within the individual as the prefix intra, which means within, suggest. The second instance of a one-sided communication is not as fruitful as the first one. If I may put it, the second instance takes a 360-degree turn from intrapersonal personal communication since no exchange happens at all though it may involve two or more people. This is known as communication breakdown. Having an exchange classified as such is very unfortunate for everyone involved. It is so because the actual communication process does not occur – messages and responses are not delivered fully to drive the result that is initially intended by the interaction.

Being aware that communication processes can fail is very important. Those people who fail to recognize this fact often have poor relationships with others which could have resulted from a tattered communication skill.

Having this book in your hands is one step away from suffering such consequences that you don't deserve in the first place. Here, you will get a holistic view of public speaking from its roots up until it becomes your second nature. Each page is filled with tips, trick and inside information that can help you unleash not only the power speaker but even the more powerful communicator in you.

Reading this first page has already opened the door to your success in many endeavours. You may not become a millionaire or a royalty in a bat of an eyelash but you can surely take control of many circumstances in your life if you can articulate well. Being able to do powerful presentations as well as deliver heart warming messages during important occasions can help you build a better life and keep it that way. But before you bask in the glory of the communication skill that you'll learn or enhance in this book, please remember this one important principle from the Greek philosopher Epictetus – **We have two ears and one mouth so that we can listen twice as much as we speak.**

Communicating, especially with a large number of people, is not only about words and endless talk. It is also about listening – of seeing, understanding and delivering needs in order to complete a full cycle.

Reading through the pages of this book is child's play. But unlike anything easy, it'll be well worth it.

Chapter 1: Assuming A Dancing Position

People who turn words into money are big thinkers! They know exactly that words are assets, and too often they have use it to achieve their aims – wealth, riches, success, health, friendship, relationship, love, business, cordiality – you name it!

The art of turning words into money, therefore, is a gift that has been entrusted into the care of each and everyone of us right from Creation. The problem, however, is that most of us think we don't have what it takes, that we don't have that capacity to make it happen!

To be honest, turning words into money means knowing what some people don't know, seeing what some people can't see, and then by passionately talking about it, organizing a conference, seminar or a talk show and charging a fee!

And do you know what? That is precisely what writers, journalists, newscasters, radio and TV presenters does on a regular basis, only that a lot of us don't seem to understand and see it that way.

The only difference between them and the average Joe or Josephine on the street is because their kind of speaking business has been intricately and highly glorified; they'd used the concept and the power of image creation to project their ventures, to make it a global, glorified empire and to make it look lager than life!

And the truth is, unlike them you don't have to be a writer, a journalist, a newscaster, a radio or TV presenter before you can earn from what you know!

Therefore the path to the creation as well as to the success of this bussiness is, first and foremost, to learn how to always **assume a dancing position with your target audience,** assuming you have successfully defined what you really wanted, what you're good at, what you are passionate about and are willing to take it to the next level!

So what do I mean with the word, **assuming a dancing position?** I'll explain.

What Maintaining a Dancing Position Really Means

In the book of Luke 19:1-5, there was no doubt from the scriptural account given by St. Luke that **Jesus understood this concept so well. In fact, because of this He understood Zacchaeus's mindsets to the last alphabet.** He knew how embittered, frustrated and desperate Zacchaeus was in order to have an encounter with Him, hence his reason for climbing the sycamore tree!

However, for Zacchaeus to have an encounter with Jesus, for him to truly relate with the Master on a personal and intimate level Jesus had to assume a dancing position with him, too.

But how? By telling him to climb down from the tree, and making the decision to visit and stay at his house as an invited guest. This, undoubtedly, would better position the both of them, Jesus and

Zacchaeus, to get to know each other intimately.

What an incredible secret!

Although Jesus understood Zacchaeus's mindset; however if He, Jesus, must wine, dine and have an inter-personal and intimate relationship with him and hence, change his negative lifestyle and perception to life, He must also assume a dancing position with Zacchaeus!

This, certainly, is one of the best ways by which He can have access and positively impact his lifestyle and change his perception; and He did that so well! He did maintained that dancing position!

Furthermore, the same could be said of Apostle Paul, the man who had been argued to be the greatest marketing genius in the Christendom. Because Apostle Paul understood this concept and the importance of maintaining a dancing position with your target audience, he succeeded far more than what most of us could possibly think.

Little wonder he affirmed to the fact that to the weak he was weak; to the Jew he was a Jew; to those under the law as being under the law; and to those who live without law he acted and behaved living without law, though not without law unto God.

He made himself servant to all that he may gain all! What a perfect concept of maintaining a dancing position! Little wonder he excelled in his ministry.

The Key to Turning Words into Money

You see, the key to turning words into money is to first understand this concept of maintaining a dancing position with your partner, or the mindset of your targeting audience, the person you're either trying to talk or sell to.

To achieve that on a consistent basis you must learn how to . . .

Assume a Dancing Position with Your Audience.

How?

Perhaps we should learn from Apostle Paul who understood this concept so well when he said, "For though I be free from all men, yet have I made myself servant unto all, that I might gain the more. And unto the Jews I became as a Jew, that I might gain the Jews; to them that are under the law, as under the law, that I might gain them that are under the law; To them that are without law, as without law, (being not without law to God, but under the law to Christ,) that I might gain them that are without law. To the weak became I as weak, that I might gain the weak" **(I Corinthians 9:19-22).**

Did you get that?

Alright, let me bring it back home now. Have you ever wondered why most telecommunication companies, especially within the Nigerian cities succeeds almost in every tariff plan they offer the public? That is because they understood your mindset! They knew you want to talk more and pay less! They knew you're willing to pay a kobo just to talk for a minute!

They knew you're willing to pay a penny to chat for some seconds! They knew you're desperate to send endless test messages at a very low prices! They knew you want quality service for a dime!

No wonder they always come up with different offer and tariff plans just to suite your ego and appeal to your emotion, and in the process they'd exploited you because of your impulsive desire to communicate over the phone. And yes, they've exploited YOU!

And often times they've come with offers like . . .

1Family and Friends.

2Midnight Calls.

3Free Data plan or MB for browsing the internet either through your phone, your PC or laptop.

4Free credits (i.e. airtime units) that is almost equivalent or more than the credit unit you loaded into your cell phone.

5 Fast Internet Speed.

6 Instant airtime the minute you activate a new SIM card and so on.

One of the best ads I've ever heard amidst hundreds of radio commercials and which, believe it or not, I so much loved was the recent ads by Airtel, a telecommunication company that ran thus, **"Challenged your speed"** and, **"Speed is an attitude."**

And yes, that is the truth! **Making money is like challenging your speed and brilliant ability.** It's like making speed towards achieving your goal an attitude.

Or to put it more broadly: making money with words is like assuming a dancing position and learning to put your leg into someone else's dancing shoes without necessarily stepping on his (or her) toes to really get what you want!

And that dancing shoes could be that of your target audience, your customer, client or whoever you might be dealing with: your friends, family, loved ones, enemies, foes or your rivalries such as your political opponents, business competitors and so on and so forth.

And that's precisely what these telecommunication industries does on a regular basis. Always they are assuming your dancing position regardless of whether you know it or not. And as far as they are concern this is what they are doing, ***assuming your dancing position to get into your wallet.***

Hence they maintain this sporting position dancing Salsa dance, Wartz, Break Dance, Hip-pop, Galala, Swore and

all kind of dance that you're probably familiar with so as to gain access into your hard-earned money.

They put their legs into your dancing shoes and dance along with you without necessarily stepping on your toes!

And as they meticulously dance along, as they slowly follow your dance steps with the rythm of the beats, the only thing they continually whispers to your ears are the benefits of their products and/or services.

Ah, little wonder they've succeeded in taking your hard-earned money without you even knowing it!

They know how and where to scratch your back when it itches!

Now, how can you do the same assuming you have an interest, a passion or a hobby you're willing to monitize into a speaking business or any business of your choice?

First, you will have to find out what people want from you! And to do that as much as the big companies does you must first, as it were, put your legs into their dancing shoes and dance along with them!

Jesus understood this concept when He turned five loaves of bread and two fishes to feed thousands of people who came to hear His Words. The Bible reads, **"When Jesus then lifted up his eyes, and saw a great company come unto him, he saith unto Philip,** *Whence shall we buy bread,*

that these may eat?" (John 6:5, **Emphasis Added).**

Jesus knew they were hungry. He knew they had to be fed if they must listen to His Words. Hence He got into their shoes and danced along with them by providing them lunch after the preaching of the day.

Let me relate a personal story to further expand this concept a little.

Yars back when I was young and still growing up as a child I had the habit of hanging around my mum whenever she's in the kitchen, preparing either supper or dinner.

Now each time she gets to the kitchen and starts putting those fishes on the frying pan, what I do often was to sit close to her, carefully watching and monitoring every moves as she adds, with all of those kitchen rituals**,** the necessary ingredients to the food she's cooking.

If you were to come around in those days you would had probably thought that I'm a good, responsible lad(although that does not mean that I was a bad boy anyway). However, since I knew what I was aiming, I learnt early in life to assume her dancing position by putting my leg into her shoes and by dancing along with her.

How? Very simple:

While preparing for dinner, I will excitedly do all she asked of me without necessarily grumbling or murmuring. I'll assist her in carrying out the basins, pouring out the dirty waters into those dirty gutters, and going for an errand without necessarily, out of a child's foolishness, refuting or complaining.

While at the kitchen and as the rituals continues, I'll assist her in slicing the onions and watched over whatever she instructed me to watched over. Why? Because I was aiming at something: **I wanted to have a taste of the fried fish before it gets into the fresh stew!**

Of course, as you'll expect, I always got my way. She always bribed me with some for staying that long with her and helping her out with some of the kitchen rituals. That habit, you see, has helped build my patience and negotiating skills. It has helped developed how to assume dancing steps with others.

Now you get the message? Right!

Early in life I discovered that if I must get what I want from her, I'll have to figure out how she thinks and do whatever she asked of me, like staying with her in the kitchen, helping out with some kitchen cores, going for an errand and all of that stuff. At the end, my effort and patience always paid off!

Until you understand what people think it would be hard, very hard, regardless of the money you're willing to make from your speaking engagementfor you to really make the money.

Big companies understand this trick. They know how their customers think! So they always try to meet and fulfill their customers' needs! **They try to satisfy their**

emotion and ego! They see from the perspective of their target audience!

See Yourself as a Company, Your Audience as Your Customer

Hey, if you must get into the speaking business you must start seeing yourself as a company and your audience as customers.

You remember the story of the blind man Jesus healed when He mixed His saliva together with clay? Half way to the healing process when Jesus asked him what he saw, he said he **"saw men as trees walking!"** Whop! You can't maintain that position or concept if you want to turn words into money and be successful at it. **You must learn to see your audience not as walking trees but as dancing partners!**

Therefore to be successful by speaking in an event, or by hosting a seminar or programme on what you're passionate about goes far beyond mere words or phrases. You will have to connect with your audience physically, emotionally and psychologically if you must record great success.

Just like someone who is willing to run a successful corporation or an architect trying to erect a skyscraper, you must have a blue print of what you want to talk about, how you want to talk about it, where it would be right and appropriate for you to talk about it, the objective of what you want to talk about, your listening audience, the benefits, how you intends to provide it and etc.

You need to know who will be present at the conference so you can use the right words to inspire and motivate, and to generate response that would favor both you and your audience.

 "But what saith it? the word is nigh thee, even in thy mouth, and in thy heart: that is, the word of faith, which we preach" **(Romans 10:8).**

You see, until you know your listening audience and know what they really want, talking at their level will be very difficult and would hardly produce result.

Chapter 2: Importance Of Public Speaking

As mentioned earlier, communication takes place between two people, a group of people, and even in one's self. If this is so, why is there a need to speak in public? Why can't we just talk to people individually? This chapter will talk about the importance of public speaking and the situations that require it.

Public speaking is important because it is an efficient way of relaying information. By speaking in public, a speaker would not have to spend so much time and effort to talk to people one by one. It disseminates a lot of knowledge at once, informing a large number of people without having to spend too much. It saves time, energy, and effort.

On a practical level, being a good public speaker is an edge when you go into the business world. Speakers, who are good at informing, persuading, and entertaining people, capture the eye of company owners. You are the kind of employee that they want to have. You are an asset because you have the skills that could satisfy their clients. Companies prefer employees who are good public speakers.

Public speaking gives credibility to a speaker. If you are asked to speak in front of a crowd, it gives your audience an impression that you are someone, and whatever you will say matters. People consider you as reputable and influential. Even if it gives you a certain sense of fear at first, eventually it will help you build and boost your self-confidence. When you are speaking in public, people will listen to you. Thus, you have the chance to tell them your opinions and beliefs. If you are able to deliver it properly, there is a high probability that the audience will believe you.

When you finally get the hang of public speaking, you will tend to be more comfortable around large numbers of people. When you are already get used to communicating with the crowd, it is now easier for you to socialize, even if the people around you are strangers. Through regular practice and enhancement, public speaking will eventually become natural to you. You will learn to speak in public without having to be afraid or nervous anymore. Public speaking does not only boost one's self-confidence, it also enhances their social skills.

The skills required in being an effective public speaker are applicable not only when one is delivering a speech, but also in many different aspects of life. For example, public speaking requires confidence. You don't just need confidence during public speaking, it is also useful when you decide to take on a risks or a new venture. Confidence is necessary when you deal with people you do not know. Being equipped with such skill will help you in your career, in your relationships, and in many activities in your every day life.

In general, public speaking is important because it is an efficient way of communicating knowledge between speakers and audiences. It gives credibility and reputation to a speaker because he or she is deemed knowledgeable on whatever topic that he or she is talking about. Public speaking becomes an avenue for speakers to show what they have and what they know, which can be factors that contribute to their promotion in their respective careers. It equips them with the necessary skills that they will need in their daily life, and helps them to have a sense of betterment and usefulness in themselves. Most of all, being able develop the characteristics of an effective public speaker is important because public speaking is inevitable. There is and will always be a point in one's life when he or she will have no other choice. The purposes, kinds of audiences, topics, and other factors may vary, but one will always have to face the task of speaking in public.

This chapter ends in a conclusion that public speaking is truly important. However, despite its importance, many people are still not willing to engage themselves in public speaking. The primary reason is fear. People are afraid to be faced with a large number of people, and more so, to speak to them. Why is this so? Why do some people fear public speaking? These questions will be addressed in the next chapter.

Chapter 3: How To Use Eye Contact

Do you find it surprising that eye contact is the first topic in a book about Public Speaking? Yet, the choice is not fortuitous because eye contact is crucially important.

Put yourself in your audience's shoes and imagine a speaker who, while talking to you, turns his gaze elsewhere. He looks at your shoulder, he looks over your head, he looks at the floor, he looks at the ceiling, he looks at someone else ... he looks everywhere, but he does not look at you!

How do you feel or what do you think, in such a situation? You are likely to have some doubts about that person and his sincerity; you wonder if he really believes in what he is talking about, if he really knows his topic ...

These are all good reasons to consider the suggestion to look into your audience's eyes. And the most important reason is that eye contact confers and communicates authority and influence.

But there's more.

Imagine talking to your audience with a blindfold. In this way you can't see -and therefore you are not aware - if people are facing you or not. You do not know if they are listening. You do not understand - and this is even more important - if the effect you want to create in them by your words (to enthral, to move, to entertain them, etc. ...) has been achieved or not.

Not looking at your audience while speaking in public - and eye contact is the most effective way to do so - is like having a blindfold. In actual fact, you lose the effect of your words and run the risk of continuing your speech until the end without realizing if what you said had an effective impact on the listeners or if you had any other kind of influence.

So, eye contact plays a key role in Public Speaking and it is vital that you take the utmost attention to this aspect.

If you maintain eye contact with your audience, they will see you as sincere, credible, honest, knowledgeable and, above all, authoritative. All these perceptions have a huge impact on the message you want to transfer to your listeners and their willingness or desire to accept it.

So, while you talk in public, look at people in their eyes! Here are some tips on how to do it.

Do not just twirl your eyes; look directly at a person, maintain eye contact with that person for a few seconds - usually three, if less your eye contact is likely to be perceived as "a shifty look" and if more it can embarrass - then pass on to another person.

Make eye contact evenly, without preference - even if the temptation is strong – for people or groups who seem to listen more attentively or to have more fun.

If your audience is small, you can make eye contact with each person.

If your audience is large, break it mentally into six sectors and look for the crucial three seconds just at one "central" person of each sector near to you at your left, at the centre and at your right. Then again look at just one person of each sector away from you at your left, at the centre and at your right.

In this way all the people in each sector will have the impression that you have turned your eyes exactly to them!

And now, some practical advice to improve even more. Get your performance evaluated by someone who knows you and who you admire and trust (you could ask more than one person). Ask them, on a scale of (1 never), (2 rarely), (3 sometimes), (4 often), (5 always):

- do I keep eye contact with people when I speak?

- is the duration of the eye contact appropriate - neither too quick nor too long?

- do I look at my audience evenly and without preferences?
- do I keep eye contact with the people who are to my left, centre, and to my right, both close to me and far from me?

In this way you can easily identify your strengths and areas for improvement, and make plans for your personal development.

Chapter 4: How To Beat Your Glossophobia

Beating any phobia takes a lot of hard work and patience. You may come to a point wherein you want to give up, but it would be better for you to keep a stiff upper lip and continue. In this chapter, you will learn about the initial steps on how you can get over (or at least minimize) your glossophobia or any phobia for that matter.

Facing your fears

The first step in getting over any irrational fear is to find out what is causing it. Most people who are suffering from glossophobia had traumatic experiences that caused them to become fearful of public speaking.

For instance, a student who tried to speak up in front of the class suddenly forgot what he or she actually wanted to say, which then drew snickers from his or her classmates. If you were just a witness to this event, then you wouldn't think much of the stifled laughter from the other students, but if you were in the embarrassed student's shoes, you would feel like those laughs pierce through your soul and make you believe that you are stupid.

Overanalyze the cause of your fears and rationalize your way out

A good way to reduce the sting of your fears somehow is to analyze the heck out of it. You probably had quite a number of sleepless nights because you kept on remembering your embarrassing slip up, when you last tried to speak in public (which may be years ago), and you keep playing that scene in an endless loop in your mind.

Do not waste your energy trying to remember the things you did wrong? Instead, you should use your mental facilities to overanalyze the incident. Take the example of the stymied student mentioned earlier; if you were a student, and the incident happened more than ten years ago, how many of your former classmates remembers it? In fact, how many of your old classmates are you still in contact with, right now?

Most of the time, the reasons for your fears are so petty until you just need to overanalyze your fears to realize it.

Be prepared

A lot of people are afraid of speaking in public, because they think that their minds will go totally blank, and they will forget everything that they need to say. The best way to counter this is to prepare before going out there.

Say your boss assigned you to make a 30-minute presentation for your next office meeting next week, don't waste time and start preparing for your presentation that very instant. The first thing to do is to gather all the materials you will need and start planning out your presentation.

It will be very unlikely that you will remember an entire week's worth of planning the moment you step in front of your co-workers. On the other hand, if you put off your preparations for the night before your big meeting, couple that with your crippling fear of public speaking, and you will certainly have a disastrous performance.

Here are some pointers on how you can better prepare yourself when you are supposed to speak in front of an audience:

You should practice in front of a mirror. Seeing yourself as you give your speech will help you find out which parts of your delivery needs more work.

Record your speech. Almost all cell phones nowadays have a camera with video recording capabilities, so you use yours to record your speech and watch it repeatedly until you fix your more noticeable quirks.

Look for local clubs or organizations that can help you improve. There are clubs like

Toastmasters who are more than willing to help their members improve upon their public speaking prowess; seek them out, and ask for their help.

Don't try to please everyone

One of the biggest reasons why people are so afraid of public speaking is because they try to please everyone in the audience. Sometimes, they have this false notion in their heads that in order for their speech to become a success, they must get the entire audience on their side, which is absolutely false. Some people even think that they need a standing ovation afterwards.

If you see someone yawn, or if you see a couple of people look bored with your speech, try to divert your attention away from them as much as you can. Chances are those people will get bored no matter who is speaking in front of them, that or they may just be tired and are unknowingly acting bored.

The truth is it's hard to please everyone, every time. It does not matter how small or large your audience is; there are bound to be at least one person who will not agree with your opinion. So don't even think about impressing everyone with your speech because it is virtually impossible for you to do so, and aiming for the impossible will only lead to failure.

It's not all about you

You have a chance to speak in front of other people because your opinion matter. Just remember, you will be delivering a speech not performing at a talent show, so don't worry about the audience judging you.

To help you get over your fear more effectively, look at your situation from a different perspective. Instead of dreading how your audience will feel about your presentation, think of them as being grateful that you were gracious enough to share your knowledge with them. Instead of thinking that you are the "star of the show", see yourself as a mere resource of information.

Speaking of being a resource of information, it is okay to admit you don't know everything, but you can still provide your audience with helpful information. Just because someone invited you to a speaking engagement, does not necessarily mean you know everything about the subject. Don't assume you are smarter than your audience because this kind of thinking is what gets many speakers in a lot of trouble.

If you don't know the answer to a particular question, it is not shameful to admit it. Just don't make it a habit of not knowing the answers to questions because it makes you just plain unprepared on your part.

Don't rush

"Let's just get this over with," shouldn't even be the way you feel when giving a speech. This kind of thinking not only makes the fear of public speaking worse, it also usually guarantees a less than spectacular speaking engagement. If you think that you can get over your fear of public speaking by rushing through your presentation, then you are mistaken.

You will make things worse for you if you try to go over your speech in record time. For one thing, if you rush your message it would only lead to you repeating most of what you said because the people in the audience did not catch them the first time.

Relax

I know that nothing gets pushes anxiety-prone people over the edge more than a person telling them to "relax", but you do need to do it. Although you cannot get rid of all your anxiety, it is important that you lessen it somewhat.

To help you relax before getting on the stage for your presentation/speech, here are some tips that you may find useful:

Get to the venue early. You should be in the venue where you will be giving a speech at least an hour early. This way, you won't be on too much of a rush to get there and add unneeded pressure on your already frayed nerves.

Walk on the stage. You are already unfamiliar with your audience so you should at least be familiar with your surroundings. You should walk around the stage where you will be giving your speech to get familiar with it, and then when it comes time to deliver your speech, your body will not feel awkward in your relatively new surroundings.

Sit in the audience's seats — Take a seat and take a look at the stage from the viewpoint of your audience. Knowing what your audience will see during your speech can help you relax and give you an idea on how you can project yourself when it's your time to talk. You can even ask a friend to walk on the stage in your place so you can get a good idea of what your audience will see when it comes time to give your speech.

Make friends with some of the people in the audience. People, who are afraid of speaking in public are also scared of talking with complete strangers. The best way to remedy this is by becoming friends (or at least acquaintances) with some people in the audience. Before your speech is to start, introduce yourself to some of the people as they come in the venue. Now, you can technically say that not all people in the room are strangers to you.

Use the "wall push technique to relax. Stand and face the wall and place your hands on it. Push on the wall, placing all of your body weight on it, as if you're doing a modified pushup. Breathe out as you push, at the same time contract the muscles in your abdomen. Repeat a couple of times until all of your nervousness go out of your body.

Take five minutes to do a bit of mindfulness meditation. Go to a quiet corner of the venue, as the stairwell, and focus your eyes on an area on the wall. As you stare at the wall and take a couple of deep breaths. You should focus your mind on your breathing, and then become mindful of everything that is going on in your body, such as the sensation on the tips of your fingers, your muscles tensing up, the light breeze touching your skin, etc. A couple of minutes of meditating like this and your mind will become calm and relax.

Fake it until you make it

Your audience will only know that you are nervous if you let them see that you are. Before you walk onto the stage, put on a face of someone who is not afraid of speaking to a crowd of people. First, pull your shoulders back, tilt your head slightly upward, and walk with a lot of confidence with a bit of a smile on your face. People will not be able to tell whether you are feeling confidence or not, so you use this to your advantage.

You should also avoid apologizing for your nervousness. As mentioned earlier, your audience most likely did not even see that you were nervous until you told them that you were. Now that your audience knows that you are near to having a heart attack because of your anxiety, you are only placing a heavier load on yourself. Instead of apologizing, you should joke about how nervous you are, this will lighten up the mood inside the room and ease some of your nerves.

Continue pretending your un-nervousness until such time that you notice that you are not acting anymore; that you're actually free of your public speaking phobia.

Do not expect that you will be completely anxiety-free just because you followed the tips mentioned above, especially if this is your first time trying them. However, you can expect that there will be a considerable reduction of your nervousness as compared to before. Keep using these methods until they turn into habits, and by that time the tide of your battle with fear of public speaking will turn to your favor.

Chapter 5: Practicing Correctly

- Let's talk about one of the best kept secrets of all great presenters, practice. Most people watch great speakers and think it looks effortless, it's not. It's the result of great practice, hour after hour. Yes, there are exceptions to the rule. A few lucky people can speak extemporaneously with little to know preparation at all, but that's rare. The vast majority of effective speakers practice hard. One or two run throughs is not really sufficient.

It takes more to build the cognitive and behavioral comfort required to deliver a great talk. So, let's give it a definition. Practice is a thoughtful series of rehearsals. I recommend at least five, using built-in feedback loops, resulting in clearly increased comfort and effectiveness when speaking. There really are three main benefits that explain why you have to spend time practicing. The first is painful but necessary. Practice exposes your biggest delivery flaws.

You can't fix something if you don't know it's broke. You might have some odd jargon you're using too much, or a strange nonverbal tic, that's driven by nerves, that you're completely unaware of. Now, listen, you're not trying to become perfect, no one is, but you can learn to identify your biggest quirks and errors in order to target them for improvement. The second benefit is increased awareness of how to improve the content you're delivering. You might be too heavy on numbers, or maybe you left out an important part of your argument.

Or, maybe you realize you have more time than you thought and can comfortably focus on additional details. No matter what the content tweak might be, it's during practice this becomes evident. The last huge benefit is increased comfort and confidence. The simple nature of repetition makes presenting feel more normal. The more normal it feels, the more you can take control and start making positive changes, instead of merely fretting about what others are thinking.

Few actually get rid of all nerves, but through practice you can learn to put them in check. It will show up in your more calm and smooth voice, and thoughtful nonverbal behaviors. So, let's think for just a second about how you can practice in a way that allows you to realize these benefits. First, I want you to mimic the conditions that will be present when you actually give the speech, to the extent it's possible. In fact, if you can, practice in the room where you'll actually deliver.

Next, no distractions, you want solid, uninterrupted time to practice. No phones chirping, no people walking in and out, and so on. To build a reliable routine for this speech, your practice needs to be focused. No multitasking or distractions. It's also helpful to use an actual audience. It might be one person or a handful of colleagues. Having them there makes it feel real and forces you to deal with their presence and learn to get comfortable.

If you choose well, it also means they can give you good feedback about what you're doing well, and what needs improvement. Finally, try capturing audio or video of your practice sessions. It's always brutal to watch and always very useful for making you aware of how you truly look. Practice is the cornerstone of all solid presentations. If you practice sufficient number of times and follow the guidelines we discussed, the day of the presentation will take care of itself. It's just another repetition of the quality routine you've developed.

Figuring out what works for you

- During your practice sessions, you want to do your best to find out what works for you. Through the process of watching other good speakers in person, watching videos online, and gathering best practice type of advice, just like I'm delivering in this course, but you still have to find your own unique voice. You should really look at all advice only as a good place to start thinking about yourself as a speaker. Instead of meeting every best practice, following every rule of good speaking and trying to be a perfect speaker, I want you, instead, to remember this.

You're just trying to get better on average over time. Listen to the feedback others give you. Watch the video of yourself you've collected. The goal is to identify the places in the presentation where things feel like they're working, things appear to feel natural. Now, ask the question, "Why?" Is it a particular topic you're addressing or maybe after you're done with a topic you don't enjoy. Is it a certain time during the presentation? Identify why because there's almost always an explanation.

If it's a topic you love, maybe it can be expanded. If it's a topic with which you struggle, maybe you can reduce it or change how you deal with the topic to help improve your flow. Next, I want you to do the very same thing with the places in the presentation where you were the least comfortable and natural-looking. Ask why as a place to begin thinking about changes. I don't want your list of areas to improve to be 20 items long. Three or four will do just fine. Here's what you need to remember.

Every audience member knows you're imperfect, and they don't expect perfection. They expect you to get a preponderance of the variables correct. We've got the actual content you're delivering, your nonverbals, voice control, and all the other variables we've addressed before. You've got to get two-thirds to three-quarters of them correct, so you're really only looking to leverage or embellish one or two things and fix or improve two or three things. That's how you get past the average person's threshold of acceptance so they can simply focus on your message.

Let me get you started as simply as possible. When you think about what works for you and what doesn't, just try to identify one thing you can start doing that you're currently not doing. One thing you have to stop doing that isn't productive and one thing you can change a little to improve how you do it. That's it; start, stop, change. When you add the benefits of practice and repetition on top of that, you're on your way. No speaker is perfect, but we can all be more effective, and that begins with identifying where you're currently most effective and comfortable and why.

Then you can use that to improve the rest of the presentation, too. That way, the final product really does showcase your best presentation skills.

Chapter 6: Symptoms Arising From Fear Of Public Speaking

Most people experience public speaking anxiety when they are called upon to speak in public: others panic merely at the thought of being called upon to speak in public. Some people even deliberately avoid events if they think there is the slightest possibility that they might be called upon to speak. Others promise themselves they will never speak in public. But, as we are social beings, we all need to interact with each other and the day will surely come when we have to speak before a crowd or a group of people. This is particularly so for those in the public arena, such as leading businessmen and politicians. A leader cannot avoid speaking in public.

There is no definite science to help overcome the fear of public speaking, but there has been some scientific research into the symptoms associated with it. Researchers have found that some people experience both physical and verbal symptoms. The symptoms are said to act as a defence mechanism, whereby, the sympathetic part of the Automatic Nervous System reacts in dangerous or stressful situations with a 'fight or flight' response. Because the sympathetic system operates on an all-or-nothing-basis, adrenaline secretion produces a wide range of symptoms all at once. These symptoms are all supposed to enhance one's ability to fight or escape a dangerous situation. It is the intensity of the 'fight or flight' response that causes verbal and physical symptoms. Verbal symptoms include a tense voice, a quivering voice and vocalised pauses. This speech anxiety prevents the speaker from communicating effectively but tends to comfort anxious speakers. Common physical symptoms are increased heart rate, increased perspiration, increased oxygen intake and stiffening of neck and upper back muscle. Of course, it is important to realise that the solution lies in taking steps to deal with the fear of speaking in public, which is the cause of these symptoms.

The Causes of Public Speaking Anxiety

Fear can arise from a person's inability to think of a logical or practical way to deal with adversities or difficulties. There are many reasons why people are fearful of speaking in public. The tendency is to worry about things that might go wrong but, in reality, never do. I will discuss here some of the most common reasons why so many people feel fearful about speaking in front of a group or crowd of people. Some worry that the audience will find their speech boring. Others worry that they will make a mistake during their speech and look foolish in front of others. Public scrutiny is also source of a lot of anxiety for many. There is often a presumption on the part of speakers that the audience is carefully scrutinising them and judging their performance. This causes some people to worry that they may have to endure shame and embarrassment should they not live up to expectations. Such negative thoughts are often triggered by the memory of past mistakes and also by uncertainty. Uncertainty as to how things will turn out on the day is the cause of much anxiety and stress.

It's natural for a person to feel a little nervous about speaking in public but it need not be a cause of anxiety or stress. Likewise, making a mistake during a speech is nothing to be fearful about, nor should it be a cause of anxiety or stress. Knowing what is expected and preparing well are key factors in eliminating these concerns. Fear is worry magnified. The effect of worrying is that any concerns that a person may have are magnified and will often appear worse or more serious than they really are. The anxiety caused by worry only serves to divert one's attention away from the real purpose of achieving their objective. This is a distraction, which causes one to loose track of a good train of thought or the ability to focus. So, relax and try not to dwell on unrealistic fears. Instead, focus on the positive aspects of your situation. Most importantly, draw on your inner strength to help you cope with your situation. Reflect on your past achievements and the personal qualities that helped you to succeed in the past. Then focus on how you can make your performance a success, so that you can achieve the outcome you desire. A useful coping technique is to practice to concentrate in order to achieve the right mental state: this will help you to concentrate on what you say, rather than what people may think about your speech. A beginner's course in meditation would be useful in this respect. Finally, be self-supportive. Tell yourself that you are in control of the situation and that you are doing a good job and remind yourself of your most admirable qualities.

Chapter 7: Begin To Reduce The Fear Or Eliminate It Completely

After doing some soul-searching, how do we continue to reduce our anxiety and fear of public speaking? Maybe no one around is hostile, nor are we. Maybe it is a fear we were born with. Well, don't worry. I have a few tips that have helped me become a better presenter; I hope they work for you, too, and help you succeed in school and in life in general.

Tip Number One: Read

When we are speaking to others, in small groups and maybe individually, say, with a girl or boy we like, we might make a fool of ourselves by not finding the right words to say. We'll have racing thoughts, our brains hurriedly running through all the words registered in it as it tries to locate the appropriate ones to use. But sometimes this proves to be a difficult feat, and were left with simple, boring, one-syllable replies like, "Yeah; Okay; or Me too." If we are conversing with the person we like, or a potential employer, and fail to find the right words to create a lively discussion, we just blew a chance at dating them, or potentially landing our dream job. It is imperative to not find ourselves with nothing to say. As we well know, a first impression makes a lasting impression; so, we have to make it count.

How do we reduce the chances of stumbling when speaking to an individual or presenting to a group of students? By reading. Yes, plain old reading. Try to read as much as possible. Try to read at least half an hour to an hour a day. Reading helps build your vocabulary; thus, your brain has more to choose from. It's like bowling: You're likely to hit a pin when all ten pins are up, not when there's only two erected. Same with public speaking and interacting with others: You're likely to find the right words if your vocabulary base is vast and broad. So, read, read,

read. You'll find yourself using words you wouldn't normally use before you started a reading regimen. It is not about sounding fancy with huge words, but being familiar with enough words to easily construct meaningful sentences. Our confidence to speak publicly will gradually increase as we read and our vocabulary rests on a solid foundation. Your school presentations will become slightly easier to deal with. You'll gain confidence in yourself after every successful, meaningful conversation with fellow students or peers. Slowly you'll break out of your shell.

But, to eventually become comfortable presenting in school and talking to others, you'll have to do more.

Tip Number Two: Research

Research. This ties in with reading. If your professor requires you to present, for example, on the US Supreme Court (USSC), don't just read the class material and expect to deliver an exquisite presentation. The bare minimum will make your presentation extremely difficult to conduct.

To present on the (USSC) and do well on it, you have to read, read, and…read. You have to become very familiar with the topic; you have to indulge in literature about the USSC. Similar to building your vocabulary and allowing yourself to find the right words, reading on the subject will allow to discuss many things about it. You'll soon realize you'll need more time than just the 5 to 10 minutes your professor gave you. Why? Because a student may ask a question, and you'll likely be able to address it after having prepared very well for the presentation. And in the process of addressing that question, it might lead to other discussions and so on; having abundant knowledge on a topic will drastically improve your confidence, because you'll likely never be without anything to say. Almost anything any student says, you'll be able to tie it to something you learned while conducting thorough research on the topic.

When we present to students and other groups, we also fear our information is incorrect. Proper preparation and research will greatly reduce the chances of providing incorrect information, or being corrected on the spot by our teacher or professor. Our presentations will flow like a river down a hill, without any embarrassing interruptions. If you take the time to prepare, you'll deliver good presentations. After each one, you'll feel more comfortable presenting. Like anything else: it takes practice.

While you are conducting research for a presentation, however, always be diligent to map out your presentation. Break it down into sections. For example, include an introduction, then discuss what legal document established the USSC. Then discuss where the USSC gets its authority from. And after that, discuss why it is important. The way you map out your presentation depends on how and on what your professor or teacher wants you to present on. Nevertheless, always map out your presentation and practice before you present. It helps to stay on track if you split the presentation into manageable sections. You'll soon realize, after every successful presentation, that it gets easier. Trust me.

So, remember, read up on the subject as much as possible; your presentation will be fluid and halfway through you'll enjoy it.

Tip Number Three: Hand gestures

In this section I discuss, not something involving intellectuality, but our physical bodies. When I present, I like to use hand gestures. I find that hand gestures relief some of the tension. Try it.

Some people suggest not to use hand gestures, to stay put during a presentation. Even though some people frown on hand gestures, it is the wrong advice to give to someone with the fear of public speaking.

Moving our hands, physically expressing ourselves, helps with the anxiety and tension we feel when presenting. To avoid hand gestures will adversely affect presenters wary of their poor public speaking ability. It's like asking someone who feels like crying to hold it in. It's better for someone on the verge of crying to let it out. Release some of that tension that we feel presenting to classmates and other groups of people by utilizing your body and not suppressing its movement. Let the body express itself freely.

Tip Number Four: Always speak loudly and clearly

Nothing indicates your level of nervousness more than speaking softly. If there's one thing that helps our fear of public speaking, it is that others don't know about it. If people don't know we have this fear, they won't think about it or scrutinize us for it. Thus, even if we are nervous and anxious, we must always remember to speak loud and clear. That gives the impression we are confident and we demonstrate we have authority speaking on the subject we are presenting on. We impose ourselves onto listeners and demand their attention and respect.

If we are timid and quiet, we will seem hesitant and unprepared. That is not the impression we want to give to anyone we want to impress, especially teachers and professors who give us our grades. You never know; you just might score high by simply presenting with confidence and authority. Your outward appearance can carry you far. But, don't just rely on that. Make sure you are prepared. Preparation, speaking clearly and loudly, with authority, will help you follow through with presentations and boost your confidence.

Chapter 8: Strategies And Techniques You Can Use

Now, remember all those signs that you may have **Glossophobia,** as discussed in the first chapter? Well, those signs can also mean that you have developed greater anxieties such as the Social Anxiety Disorder (SAD). If you think that your speech anxieties cause you to, for example, switch college courses or jobs just to avoid public speaking opportunities then you might need therapy and counseling aside from taking advantage of the solutions detailed in this book. Of course, you could still apply the following techniques to calm you or regain your sense of purpose, but individuals with SAD are highly encouraged to see a professional regarding their condition.

As for the people who simply have mild speech anxieties and fears, you can try out the techniques discussed below, and see which one of them works for you. The techniques here are aimed to lessen the physical, verbal, and non-verbal manifestations of your speech anxieties. They should help you to perform better or deliver your speeches with more confidence and clarity.

A Simple Breathing Exercise

Having better control of your breathing means that you can control your doubts and fears—how fast or slow you breathe shows how your body is feeling. Slow, even breathing suggests calmness, while rapid or uneven breathing suggests panic. Being calm before, during and after any speech performance will certainly help you perform better.

Step 1: Before your performance, look for a quiet area where you can sit and meditate. Some people find it possible to do breathing exercises while they are in the presence of the audience. They become desensitized to the noise and the people. Pick a place which suits you. Sit down and gather your thoughts.

Step 2: Start the exercise by inhaling deeply. If you feel comfortable enough, you can close your eyes. If not, then you can always focus on something or someone. Look at the stage or a person you trust and make that your focal point.

Step 3: Exhale very slowly. Feel the air leave your lungs. Do not get distracted by anything or anyone.

Step 4: Inhale again. This time, assure yourself that you are calm, that your fears of public speaking can be conquered, and that you will be absolutely fine on stage or on the podium.

Step 5: Exhale for the second time. Release all your doubts, anxieties, and fears. Do not let them bother you anymore.

Repeat steps 4 and 5 as many times as you want, or until you feel yourself become physically and mentally calm.

During your speech, if you feel like you are about to break out in sweat, or that you are about to lose track of what you are saying, inhale and exhale as evenly as you can. You can also pause for a while and count to ten. Never mind that you lost a few seconds of momentum with your speech. The important thing at this stage is that you are able to calm yourself, and get back into your speech without any anxiety plaguing you.

After your speech, if you suddenly feel nervous or if your hands begin to shake, repeat the steps for the breathing exercise until you regain composure. Once you achieve a state of peace, reward yourself. If you were able to control your panic attacks or your fears of public speaking, then you have reached a milestone in your journey to be a better speaker.

Here are other techniques to conquer your anxieties and fears of public speaking, and become a better speaker.

Avoid the caffeine!

Do not drink coffee before you deliver a speech. Aside from affecting your vocal chords, caffeinated products tend to increase anxiety and they also often ruin your calm energy level because of high doses of sugar. If you want to drink something before meeting your audience, then choose an herbal tea, or better yet just get a glass of lukewarm water.

Exercise before you speak.

Another good way to rid yourself of the butterflies in your stomach before your speech is to exercise early in the morning. This way, your body is allowed to release pent up energy and frustration in a natural and healthy way. Exercise also helps clear the mind and makes the body feel generally better.

Dress the part you need to play.

Nothing says confidence like a handsome suit or a stunning dress. Choose clothes that are appropriate for both the topic of your speech and the occasion. Male speakers would do well to add a bowtie or tie to their attire, especially if they are attending a formal dinner or meeting. Female speakers need not wear extra high heels, but they should add a few accessories that draw the audience's attention to the speaker's face and what she is saying. Dress the part you need to play. Both you and your audience will benefit from this simple technique to vanquish public speaking fears. You see, your audience will be more likely to accept and respect you if you dress well, and you will feel more confident and graceful if you know that you look good.

Practice makes perfect—or at least, helps you become better at what you are supposed to do.

This is the technique all professional public speakers know and use all the time. If you are particularly afraid of speaking to a large assembly, or if you hate having to stand on the stage with a spotlight trained on your every move, then practicing your speech is the best way to help you overcome those anxieties. Constant practice helps you focus on the content of your speech. It eliminates the need for cue cards and frees your hands for better gestures. It also helps you gain confidence. If you practice consistently before your speech, then you will have an easier time remembering what to say, how to say it, and what to do to help the audience understand your message.

Create a schedule for practicing your speech skills, and stick to it.

Make sure you have time to practice, not only your speeches, but your delivery, tone and volume of your voice, your gestures and your movements. You can start small at first, and then gradually work your way up to longer speech drill sessions.

For example, on the first day of practicing your speech skills, you can allot five minutes for breathing exercises, ten minutes for pronunciation and enunciation, and five minutes for positive self-talk. After doing twenty-minute speech drill sessions daily for a week, you can then increase the duration of each session to forty minutes. You can start practicing your hand gestures, facial expressions, and the volume of your voice. As you go along increasing the amount of time you practice, you will find it easier to dedicate time to honing and sharpening your speech skills, and thus you will become more confident with what you can achieve.

Study the great public speakers, and allow yourself to be mentored by them.

Choose your favorite public speaker and learn everything you can about him or her. Look for that speaker's biography and learn how he or she became so good at speaking to enormous crowds. You'll be surprised to know that a lot of the greatest public speakers also had to deal with fears and anxieties just like you. Make their stories an inspiration for you to lean on and as motivation for you to be like them—or even greater.

Fuel yourself with positive thoughts and energy.

Before, during, and after your public speech, be sure to fill yourself with positivity. Remember that being pessimistic about yourself and your capabilities will do nothing but harm you. Celebrate who you are and who you can be. Let positive thoughts and energy combat your public speaking fears and anxieties.

Chapter 9: Public Speaking Is Easy Your Body Will Help!

When I do public speaking workshops, participants are always intrigued by the fact their bodies are so important to public speaking. This is another element we take for granted in public speaking – we may mistakenly think it is all about the voice, pronunciations and speech content. The body is a very important part of public speaking, not only with regards to posture on a stage, body language or gesticulations.

Think about it – how is your voice produced? Is it not produced in your body? What are the parts of the body involved in public speaking? Stop reading now and make a list in your notebook.

How many body parts did you write down? Did you write down any of the following?

mouth, teeth, nose, lips, tongue, lungs, windpipe, diaphragm, larynx, pharynx, oral and nasal cavities, nostrils, brain

While your body registers fear and nervousness, shaking hands and voice, weak knees, stomach butterflies, heart racing, palms sweating, the truth is that your body is more than well equipped to serve you well in your public speaking activity! Once you make the connection and understand this process your body will begin to support you in becoming a confident speaker.

If you wrote down fear of nervousness as one of your public speaking fears, knowing about your body in relation to public speaking will help you to overcome this fear.

Function of Body Parts in Speaking

PRONUNCIATION

TEETH

In making a note of the parts of the body in public speaking you may not have

written down 'teeth' on your list. Let me ask you to pronounce the following words without the use of your teeth by folding your
lips over them:
teeth fishfriend visitor certainzoo
Were you able to make the correct pronunciation of those words?

LIPS

You may not have written 'lips' down on your list, but let me ask can you pronounce the following words without using your lips:
mouth mother baby
brotherpush   president
post
Without your lips it would be difficult to pronounce these common English words.

TONGUE

Pronounce the following words without using of your tongue:
laughlift   linger   long
lament   Larry lazy languish

Your tongue is critical in the pronunciation of all your "L" words.

We cannot take any part of our body for granted any longer when it comes to being an effective public speaker.

TONGUE TWISTERS

Tongue twisters have been used over the ages to loosen a lazy tongue. It also helps in diction, articulation, fluency and breathing. I would definitely recommend that you spend some time at least twice per week in doing these tongue-twisting exercises that will aid you in developing your tongue muscle, and teach you control over your tongue. Make sure that you also have fun doing them.

Art awaited news of any automatic automobile affordable to him

Characters clamor creatively seeking some simple signs

Everybody wins who is honest on holidays always

Happy Helga hollered out loud Hallelujah Amen in October

This toe that tripped me twisted my foot throwing me toward the threshold of the door

SPEECH PRODUCTION

Ever wondered how speech is produced in your body?

We tend to take for granted that speech occurs when we learn to speak and begin to communicate verbally. As babies we begin to use our speaking apparatus through crying, laughing, gurgling and screaming.

However, there is a physiological process involved; your **breath** is a powerful force that supports your voice when you speak. If you are a singer you will know what this means. If you are not a singer, think about when a runner finishes a race – see how difficult it is for him or her to speak when being interviewed – he or she is out of breath.

To project your voice well is an indication of how well you use your breathing skills. The more efficiently you breathe the more air you will have to sustain your voice in projection.

Your vocal cords when they vibrate make the sound that is produced as your voice. Your breath passes through your vocal cords in your voice box located in the region of your throat. The cavities in your head and neck perform the role of resonators; they determine the tone and quality of your voice. To develop a fine tonal quality is to have a balanced use of all the resonators.

The oral cavity is manipulated by the movement of your lips, jaw and soft palate in order to change the shape of the mouth and sound into speech and words. If you were to exhale and then try to speak you would not get any sound produced as your voice. You can try it and you will experience this – as mentioned before when you are out of breath from running, you cannot speak fluently.

Breathing Exercise

Breathing is critical, not only in producing sound through your voice, but it is critical in teaching your body how not to get nervous when in any stressful situation including public speaking. This is how your body helps you to make public speaking easy.

Learn to breathe deeply and properly and you will train your body to assist you in projecting your vice, and not shouting.

Deep breathing also allows more oxygen to enter your bloodstream and consequently your brain, you will feel more alive and alert and ready to take on any challenge.

Each night before bed and each morning upon waking take ten (10) long deep breaths and experience deep calm for sleep, coming awake in the morning feeling more rested.

HOW TO BREATHE PROPERLY

Place your hands, palms down on your ribcage, inhale deeply, feeling your lungs fill with air, and your abdomen expanding along with your rib cage.

Exhale completely, allowing your abdomen to deflate, and your rib cage move inward.

Repeat 10 times, twice a day.

Once you begin to deep breathe on a regular basis, you will be calmer. This helps to lower the anxiety and worry for doing any public speaking.

Breathing is a critical focus in many forms of meditation allowing for the development of a calm spirit.

DIET AND EXERCISE

Your body is a tattletale! It tells you when there is danger, when something is wrong in your body; it

allows you to smell smoke so that you can get to safety. Your body, as mentioned before, registers your fears, preparing it to flee from danger. Public Speaking may feel like danger to many persons. The truth is no one ever dies from public speaking although persons would say so figuratively!

When you eat healthily, your body automatically performs at its best. Preparing for public speaking is similar to an athlete's preparation to run 100 metres. A healthy body supports effective public speaking! When you do not feel good in your body is shows in your posture, your facial expressions and in your gestures.

When you have a healthy body speaking to audience they connect with your confidence and high energy, giving you winning support as a presenter. Consistently improve your eating habits for optimum health and you will gain more confidence, when you feel better about yourself.

Exercise is a modern day buzz word and many persons still have not submitted to this critical element to create complete well-being. Simply walking for 30 minutes each alternate day will help to create a body that will support you in the quest of

being a better public speaker. When you feel healthy and strong, you will automatically walk with your head held high, your will walk with a powerful gait, your speech delivery posture will be commanding and you will feel comfortable with so many eyes staring at you!

Immediately you begin to see how to overcome the fear of being scrutinized or looked at – once you feel good about yourself, then certainly you will not mind getting all the attention in the world!

Chapter 10: Memory

Remember, Remember

An often overlooked worry of public speakers and presenters is simply the memorisation of large chunks of text or information that they have to speak about. The dread of forgetting a speech in front of a group of people drives many to desperation as they frantically try to 'cram' the night before a presentation.

Cramming can end in disaster - it stresses you out, and can have the opposite effect you're aiming for. Speeches that have been hastily memorised the night before can seem rushed, impersonal, and disconnected. This is because you're focusing so hard on remembering your words that you pay no attention to the speech's actual delivery.

Now, who has this problem on a larger scale? That's right, actors! Bad actors cram their lines the night before a performance, and end up risking public humiliation. This section details some of the methods good actors use for remembering their lines, that anyone can use!

First Things First

The most important thing to point out is also the most logical: the more time you give yourself to remember something, the more easily you will remember it. Remembering your lines should be the first thing you do when preparing, not the last!

It starts with reading. If you're writing your speech or presentation yourself, type it up and print it out so you have it in front of you. If you're presenting facts or a case in a courtroom or mooting situation, lay out all of the details you need to memorise, and read them, over and over again.

Sir Anthony Hopkins, arguably one of the greatest speakers of all time, famously reads his scripts exactly 100 times before he speaks a word of them. A bit extreme you might think, but it clearly works. If you want to look like you own every word you're saying, and give the impression that you're in control, then take the time to learn the words properly. Do a Hopkins!

1. Night-time Reading

Getting lines to sink in is a nightmare. Even if you don't have to memorise every word of it like an actor with a script, it will always look better if you aren't constantly referring to notes. An extremely effective way of getting information to filter into your brain is to read the words before you go to sleep at night. This way they rest in your subconscious mind overnight and are much easier to recall in the morning.

The reading shouldn't be a passive process though, you should actively rehearse the speech instead of reading it quietly like a book.

It can also help to record your words on a dictaphone or similar device (most phones have memo recorders), and listen to them before bedtime. Again you should actively pay attention and not drift off to sleep while listening to yourself.

2. Gesture Learning

This exercise is connected with the gesture exercises in the Status section.

Rehearse your speech or presentation using gesturing, but instead of the subtle, moderated gestures outlined in the Status section, make the gestures huge (see photo) and do a different movement on almost every word. Also speak the words with a strong inflection and a different intonation on each word. You might feel stupid doing this, but it can help you to embody your speech and memorise the words by making them more colourful.

Try to think of a different gesture and intonation for each word, isolating them and their importance, even words like 'the', 'and' and 'but'. This will create a more vivid memory of each word in your mind. We use this for memorising more difficult text like Shakespeare, as each word is given importance.

Repeat the exercise but half the intensity and the frequency of the gestures, then keep repeating until you have minimised the speech to a normal, presentable manner.

3. Line by Line

This is a tip that will help to give your speech structure, and give you a visual method of learning the words.

Type up your speech and separate each and every sentence with double spacing.

Print it out.

You should have something similar to the way this passage is formatted.

Now cover up every line but the first with a piece of paper.

Repeat the first line over and over again until you no longer have to look at the page.

Reveal the next line and repeat the first line, then add on the second line until you can remember both lines.

Go down the whole speech in this way, and it will start to sink in!

Breaking speech down into manageable sections is a great way of memorising it.

If you try to take on too much at once, it can be overwhelming and you will give up easily - but splitting it into sentences will make it easier to digest.

This method will also let you know whether some of your sentences are too long, as you'll be able to physically see them in comparison to others.

4. Multitask

Once you get to a point where you can pretty much remember the main points of your speech, try this:

As you go about your everyday activities; simple things like cleaning, cooking, getting dressed, etc, try to recite your speech. Trying to remember it whilst engaged in another activity will really embed it in your mind and it will make it much easier to recall when it comes to the actual presentation or speech.

If you need to have a look at your notes, go ahead. Don't beat yourself up, just remember where you lost the speech and put a strong emphasis on the first word you forgot. This will highlight it in your mind for next time.

And Don't Forget...

Trying to remember a lot of information is hard on your brain, and it takes time to sink in. If you expect to be able to sit down for 2 hours and remember even a 10 minute, you'll probably be disappointed.

I suggest working on it in 15 minute chunks. Read your speech, record, listen to it and repeat it, use Gesture Learning or the Line By Line technique, however you choose to do it, but only attempt it in short, regular bursts.

This is much more effective, and easier on you and your brain than trying to tackle it in one go. It's just like exercise, you need periods of rest in between the work to allow the words to filter into your mind, just like you rest between exercising to let your muscles recover.

Chapter 11: Perfection: The Great Enemy

The prospective speaker often worries about delivering what he says is a good speech. What he's actually worrying about is that he wants to deliver a **perfect** speech. Humans being humans and therefore fallible, this is quite obviously a rather difficult task to achieve.

To paraphrase the words of the great speaker and Prime Minister Winston Churchill, as in the quote above: **Bollocks to that.**

Instead, take some inspiration from him and his contemporary monarch, King George VI. Both had speech impediments, with the King notably having a stammer that he dealt with only with the assistance of Lionel Logue, an Australian speech therapist.

Churchill's impediment still remains under debate, but he definitely had one, whether a lisp or a stutter. And yet despite this detail that would make other, lesser men quake at taking the stage, both instead delivered genuinely inspiring public addresses to the entire British Empire over the course of the Second World War.

Imagine this. You are King George VI, your stammer only recently brought under control thanks to Logue. You're minutes away from having to give a speech that'll be heard by people from London, Inverness, Swansea, Belfast, Toronto, Cape Town, Madras, Ballarat, Auckland, and so many more other cities, people from all walks of life hanging onto your words delivered by radio.

It's radio, but it's the **entire** British Empire you're speaking to. More people would be surprised if you **weren't** feeling a deal of stage fright from that prospect.

And yet despite his stammer and the fright he must have been feeling, His Majesty delivered his first address to the Empire at the start of the Second World War, in September of 1939.

His performance was far from perfect, and it shows; the BBC has a recording of the speech in its archives, available for a listen online, and one can clearly hear the troubles he has with his diction, even with Logue's help. And yet the speech itself still works, and it **works well**.

If a stammering king could stand up and make himself heard to hundreds of thousands of people in hundreds of cities and stand up to the task despite his troubles, then you can as well.

Use perfection only as an **ideal**, and not as a **goal**. Strive for it if at all possible, but under no circumstances permit it to hinder your performance.

There is always room for improvement, but so long as you try and deliver a **good** performance, you'll never go wrong. You only need to speak; you don't need to speak perfectly.

Chapter 12: Let's Breathe

Learning to breathe correctly is one of the most important ingredients any speaker should have when building your stage.

What I'd like to do here is have you take a deep breath in. Seriously. But please if you have any lung or health conditions, check with your doctor first.

On the count of three take a deep breath in and hold it. READY?

Here we go…

… One … Two … Three, deep breath in and hold it (4-5 seconds) … now exhale (wooooo). GOOD.

Let's do that again... This time pay attention to what happens to your chest and shoulders when you take in a deep breath. Ready ... One ... Two ... Three, deep breath in ... hold it ... and exhale...

Did your chest and shoulders rise up? Most likely they did. This is not the correct way to breathe. If you're a singer, musician, actor or professional speaker who gets it, you know what I'm talking about. When you learn to breathe correctly it is also more relaxing. As your diaphragm fills, your lungs expand out front and to the sides.

Think about what happens when you breathe in and your shoulders rise? It puts a squeezing motion on your heart and makes you more anxious, so please don't let anyone tell you breathing wrong is a good thing to do before you get up to speak.

I'm continually surprised at how many speakers don't breathe correctly. When you tell a speaker they should learn how to control their breathing … they look at you like you are saying something in a foreign language. I've heard things like: "Well, I thought that was just for singers." "I breathe just fine." Or "Is it really **that** important?"

I'm amazed that speakers don't find this one of the most fundamentally important elements in their career.

About a year ago I recall reading a blog post written by a professional speaker who does many weekend seminars and he openly admitted that he lost his voice and had to ask one of his fellow speakers to step in and finish the seminar. Why did this happen? There was no reason for him to lose his voice. But I will give him the benefit of the doubt and maybe, just maybe, he was coming down with something. You should be able to speak for hours upon hours when you breathe correctly.

If you don't have a voice left, you won't be speaking at all.

Don't leave this out of the stage you are building. If you don't have a voice left, you won't be speaking at all.

Singers, musicians and actors have learned to breathe correctly, so why not speakers? Why is there so little focus on breathing in the speaking business? When breathing is mentioned it is rarely taught in the correct manner. When you watch public speaking videos on breathing online they don't get it at all. You'll see chests and shoulders moving upward instead of outward. Not long ago I read an article that basically said, "Singers and speakers use a deep-breathing exercise to begin a song or speech …." **Begin** a song or speech? What about the rest of the song and speech. It's not just at the beginning; we must continue to breathe from our diaphragm and expand our lungs until the end of the song, performance or speech.

Breathing from your diaphragm and expanding your lungs is the correct way to breathe. For actors, it is one of the first things you learn as part of your training. We all get lazy and become lung breathers, but watch a baby sleeping or a dog lying down; they are breathing from their diaphragm, they are breathing naturally. Somewhere in life we unlearn what was naturally given to us. Breathing incorrectly makes your voice thin and tinny and puts unnecessary stress on your vocal cords. Diaphragmatic, lung-expanding breathing gives your voice a richer, fuller sound and makes your vocal cords happy

Let's look at the six benefits of breathing from your diaphragm:

1. Your voice gets support. It takes the strain off your vocal cords by causing the air to flow naturally over them. By using your diaphragmatic muscles to push the air out, you can increase your volume and save your vocal cords.

2. It makes your voice richer, fuller, more appealing and dynamic.

3. You'll find you won't be dropping endings of words or sentences because you ran out of breath.

4. It will help your sentences flow more smoothly, not only will you be able to speak longer on one breath, that breath will also bridge the pauses. A number of speakers, SPEAK IN, SHORT, CHOPPY, GROUPS OF WORDS, because they don't ... have the breath ... to support ... a full sentence ... or come to a natural break. Get my gist?

5. You should be able to speak comfortably for at least 4-6 hours when you breathe correctly and not lose your voice.

6. If you're nervous, breathing slowly and deeply from your diaphragm and expanding your lungs helps calm you, whereas taking a deep shoulder rising breath into your lungs causes more anxiety.

Breathing affects more than people realize.

Take time to listen more carefully to speakers. Do they run out of breath, do you hear them gasping for air? Is their voice rich sounding or thin and tinny? Are they dropping endings of words or sentences? Do you hear ... irritating ... patterns ... in their speech? This is a great lesson for any speaker. Breathing affects more than people realize.

Now that this has been brought to your attention, you'll start to pick up on these irritating speech patterns and you'll begin to hear endings of words or sentences being dropped because the speaker had no breath left.

Let's recap the benefits:

Your voice does not tire as fast.

It forces your vocal cords to naturally come into play and not feel strained.

You will have better resonance; your voice will be richer and easier to listen to.

Your sentences appear to be better connected, rather than sounding choppy.

Breathing correctly is a great way to help calm your nerves.

Chapter 13: Everyone Can Be A Good Speaker

You will benefit at the beginning of your speech if you free yourself from two misconceptions:

1. Effective speakers are born, not made; it is hopeless to try being one if you were not gifted with a God-given ability.

2. For most people, fear and nervousness are impossible to overcome; it is useless to even try.

Let's take a look at each of these false assumptions.

Are Good Speakers Born and Not Made?

You don't actually believe this, or you wouldn't be reading this book. Everyone is born a baby, and babies can't speak. The "born speaker" myth is an alibi for not attempting. People who believe it simply want to save their face from the disgrace speech blunder may bring. It is a fact that practice makes perfect.

A speaker is one who speaks to others for a reason. When you were two or three years old and first said, "Mommy, I need a glass of water," you were making a speech. Actually you've been making speeches from the time you could talk; the difference is that you didn't treat it then as what you now dreadfully call "speech."

You can become a good speaker if you have these tools:

1. A voice.
2. Basic language construction: i.e., a working vocabulary and grammar.
3. Something to say.
4. A need to express your ideas to others.

You have been using these tools for years. You have been saying something to others, several times everyday, and under these conditions, you call it "conversation."

Conversation is talking to a few. Public speaking is, essentially, talking to a larger group.

Your audience is merely a group of individuals. You can talk easily with one or two individuals. So just think of public speaking as talking to individuals all at the same time - or talking to the group as to one person.

Can You Conquer Fear?

There are three solutions to help you reduce fear and make it work for rather than against you:

1. Accept it as nature's way of helping you. You don't need to be terrified of fear when you accept it as nature's way of protecting you and helping you. Recognize it. Don't condemn yourself for having it. We all feel fear. Whether your fear stems from the thought of standing alone by yourself on stage before hundreds of people, or even from the thought of getting upstage to speak, keep in mind that you are responding normally.

Athletes are nervous before an important competition; musicians tremble before a concert; performers experience stage fright. Seasoned speakers never get rid of apprehension before speaking, nor do they want to. An experienced actor once said: "I used to have butterflies in my stomach every time I stand in front of an audience. Now that I know how to make them work for me, they fly in formation."

Knowing that you are subject to a normal and common human response, you can drive out the strongest factor contributing to your fear: You can stop condemning yourself for being unusual.

Psychologists tell us that fear is not the real obstacle. We feel awkward or ineffective because we think fear is improper. It is not fear itself but your feeling about it that disappoints you. Franklin Roosevelt's note on the speech of Henry Thoreau sums it up: "We have nothing to fear but fear itself." As soon as you know this and recognize it, you are on your way to self-mastery.

Fear is nature's way of preparing you for danger, real or fancied. When you face a new or different circumstance, or when many are watching you and you don't want to mess up, nature does something great to help you, if you recognize the help rather than being disappointed by it. Nature adds the adrenaline in your blood stream. It speeds up your pulse and your responses. It increases your blood pressure to make you more alert. It provides you with the extra energy you need for doing your best. Without the anxiety there would be no extra effort. Identify fear as a friend. Recognize it and use it well.

2. Analyze Your Fear.

Your next step in mastering fear is easy and effortless. Analyze your type of fear. Fear is a tool for protection. What are you protecting? You are worried about your self-esteem. In public speaking there are only three dangers to self-esteem:

(a) Fear of yourself – fear of performing poorly or not pleasing your self-esteem.

(b) Fear of your audience – fear they may tease or laugh at you.

(c) Fear of your material – fear you have nothing sensible to say or you are not well prepared.

Fear of yourself (a) and fear of your audience (b) are very much connected. It is possible to be pleasing yourself while failing to satisfy your audience. Aiming for audience approval is often a better alternative because, if you succeed, you are in fact also pleasing yourself.

But in aspiring to satisfy your audience you must never compromise your message. Sometimes you may have to give a message to people you know are particularly opposed to it. This calls for courage. Don't fear to disagree. Good speakers have done so and have proudly walked off the stage successfully. Honest beliefs equip a speaker and give force to the speech.

3. Make use of what you have learned.

You now know that fear, nature's secret weapon, can actually help you succeed. You found you were not really afraid of fear but of yourself, your audience, and your material. Now, use your knowledge. Here's how you can:

a. Hide your negative feelings from others. If you lack self-confidence, hide it. Letting the audience know it won't help you in any way. Never discuss it. This will just make you feel worse. Act confidently. It will rub off on you. You will look the way you feel. Ever heard of the scared boy who walked past the cemetery one night? As long as he walked casually and whistled merrily he was all right. But when he walked faster, he could not refuse the temptation to run; and when he ran, terror took over.

Don't give in. Stay calm and relaxed. Enjoy your talk and your audience.

b. Assess your condition reasonably. Think of the reasons why you were called to speak. Among other possible speakers, you were chosen. Whoever asked you had confidence in you, or you would not have been chosen.

You are thought of as a competent, good speaker. And you know your topic. You know more about it than your listeners do. Your assessment reveals that you are prepared to do well and that you have the benefit over your listeners. When you accept this, your confidence will show to your audience. It will make them believe in you and in your speech.

c. Assess your audience reasonably. They want you to do well. Listeners suffer along with a speaker who is having difficulty delivering, and they do not enjoy suffering. They would much rather react and criticize; that would give them a good time. So consider your audience rather than yourself. Win their interest, and you will be more confident, and everybody will be happy.

Another way of putting this: Focus on a good message and speech delivery. You will make the audience happy with this and you will succeed in your mission. Do the first well, and the second will follow.

d. Assess your material reasonably. Fear of speech material is the easiest to conquer since the solution is simple: knowledge and preparation. Knowledge and preparation dispel fear, but by themselves they do not automatically assure the delivery of a successful speech.

A good start is when you recognize you don't need to be afraid – of yourself, your audience, or your material. And as you succeed in making speeches, you will soon say, "I can do it because I have done it often."

Nine Basic Steps in Preparing Your Speech
1. Select your topic.
2. Determine your exact purpose.
3. Identify your speech objective/s.

4. Analyze your audience.
5. Plan and organize your main ideas.
6. Organize your introduction and conclusion.
7. Prepare an outline.
8. Prepare your visual aids effectively.
9. Practice your speech

Chapter 14: Understanding Your Audience

In communication, there is something known as audience analysis. Basically, by using certain factors, you try to ascertain and gauge the perception of your audience towards the topic you are about to give. And then, you adapt your speech to suit the needs of your audience. Obviously, you cannot go around the podium or wherever it is you are giving the speech to find out who the people in your audience are individually. But there are basic things that you can use to determine how you deliver your speech in a way that is most beneficial to them. In this chapter, I am going to discuss the tools that would help you get a better understanding of your audience.

1. Size of the Audience

Now, before you get on stage, it is important that you know the capacity of the hall or podium where you been doing your speaking. This would help you determine the size of the crowd. You need this information to also help you determine the language or tone you will be using in the delivery of your speech. The general rule is that the smaller the crowd is, the more informal your speech is. So, if you are speaking to a group of 5 to 10 people, even if it is a professional setting, you can tone down the language enough to relate one-on-one in a semi formal way. As opposed to a larger crowd where things need to be kept formal even when it is an informal setting.

2. Knowledge of a Topic

You need to ask yourself, 'how well does your target audience know the topic?'. Now, it can be tricky to determine the right answer to this question, but it can be done. What you need to do is focus your research on the kind of people that will attend the event where you are doing your speaking. For instance, if you are being called upon to do a training for your colleagues, chances are, they already have basic knowledge about what you want to teach. So, you can build on this and can afford to get technical in your speech. However, if you are made to understand that these are a crowd of novices, people who have little or no idea about what you are teaching, the content of your speech should accommodate the needs of these people. Meaning that it should have foundational knowledge of the topic as well as less usage of technical terms.

3. Setting

When writing your speech to suit the needs of your audience, it is important to pay attention to where this event will be happening. For instance, if you are going to be speaking at an event that is taking place in a church, the choice of words used during your speech should honor the beliefs of the people you are speaking to so that you don't rile up anyone in the audience. This means that if you are a huge fan of curse words, you would need to apply restraint in your speech or risk losing your audience. You put yourself in a better position to appeal to your audience if you take cognizance of their values and one way to determine the value is to look at where they (your audience) are coming from or rather where they are coming to.

4. Audience Expectation

This is another tricky thing to determine, but you can get clues from the nature of the event. For instance, a comedy show means that the audience expecting anyone who comes on stage to be funny. At a memorial event, people expecting that the speaker would be sober, reflective and kind enough to offer words that are comforting and also honour the dead. Generally, you can look at the theme of the event to help you determine what the expectation of the Crowd would be. For instance, an Independence day show would mean that the crowd is expecting something patriotic and something in the line of for flag and country. Every event has a theme. Let that be your clue.

5. Audience Attitude Towards the Topic

There are three things to look at in this situation. First, you have to know if the crowd came in willingly or this was a mandatory thing. Example, if the class you are giving or doing your teaching is at an event that the company made mandatory for all there are staff, there is a very strong possibility that you would have to work harder to get their attention. As opposed to if this was an event where they show up on their own accord to attend. In the former, because you understand their reluctance, you know that you have to put in a lot more effort to gain their attention in order to make a positive impact. For the latter, you don't need to put in as much effort. You just focus on doing you the only way that you can. The second part is to understand the general perception of the audience when it comes to the topic you are sharing. Example, let us say that the focus of the speech you are giving is on a type of disease and how to manage it. There is a chance that people have always had a negative notion or false information about certain types of diseases and because this perception is widespread, it will be your duty to spend a better part of your time on stage elaborating on these myths before you get into the topic proper. Finally, you have to understand that people are generally self-centered in nature. So, whatever it is you are discussing with them, they would only be able to relate with it if you can talk about the topic in terms of how it affects them directly.

Task:

Take out the time to go on the internet and discover reliable sources that talk about tribes, religions and people of the world. You can also buy books that focus on specific cultures and read up on them. Now these topics may not be directly related to what you will be called upon to speak about. But it is essential that you know these things as they can help shape your mind in terms of how you relate with audience. Most of the insightful statements some public speakers have made in the past stems from ignorance. Do your best to educate yourself on people and showing yourself to honor the values of others even though you don't understand it.

Chapter 15: Preliminary Considerations For Your Speech

Before you start to prepare your speech, there are some factors that you need to consider ahead of time since they directly influence what you need to cover in your talk.

What Is Your Purpose

What is the purpose of your speech? Are you trying to persuade co-workers of your business plan, trying to convince people to donate money to your favorite charity, wanting to honor your brother and entertain his wedding guests? You need to have a specific goal and have this clearly in your mind as you are preparing and delivering your speech. This is a very important step, so make sure you take the time to clarify this. It is a good idea to have your goal down in writing so that you can refer to it often.

Who Is Your Audience

Your speech needs to really connect with your audience and meet their needs and expectations. If you are giving a talk on rose gardening, the content of your speech will be very different if you are giving it to a group of experienced gardeners versus a group of people who are interested in getting started with gardening. Are you talking in front of a group of business people or is it a more casual group? Really take the time to understand your audience and what information needs to be included in your speech to help them understand and connect with what you are saying. Think about what you want your audience to do and how do you want them to act after hearing your speech.

What Is The Setting

This is closely related to the audience. Is your speech going to be in a business setting, more causal environment, at a wedding? Is this going to be a large audience or a small, intimate setting?

These are also factors that affect your speech. For small groups, you will want to be more personable.

Once you have a clear idea of what your specific goal is for the speech, who your audience is and what the setting is, you can start to prepare your presentation.

However, don't skip these very important steps as part of your preparation work. It is critical that your speech tie in with your audience and the occasion. Most important of all, it is vital that you keep the goal of your speech firmly in mind while preparing your speech to ensure that your talk is a successful one that enables you to achieve your goal.

Chapter 16: The Body

We have our beginning and end to our story, and now the BODY is the main bit in the middle.

We've spoken about the three elements or golden guidelines for virtually any public 'speak' or speech.

When you have a basic understanding of this simple three-step dance, it takes some of the scary, or the mystery out of it for you.

We've covered the OPEN and the CLOSE. These are the two pieces that frame the BODY.

In the BODY of your speech, the same rules apply no matter how long or short your presentation.

OPEN – BODY – CLOSE.

So let's get down to the BODY and how to simply get there from the OPEN.

After you have said "Hello my name is Johnny Robinson ... (simple but works well, particularly if that is actually your name!) What I will be speaking about today is my experience as a New York Fireman. I would like to tell you a story about the time my fellow officers saved my life during a blaze at an apartment building in Manhattan."

Hey good open. I would love to hear about that. **What about you?**

The body then becomes Johnny telling his story.

It is simply a natural flow from the hello - to your story – and then to your close.

The easiest way to get into the story, or the BODY is to

SET THE SCENE first.

Why?

This gives your audience a mental picture. It helps to 'frame' your story or in other words, put it into some kind of context - or set up.

How would you set the scene in YOUR story?

Here is how our friend Johnny might do it.

"It happened late last year when we got a call around midnight that a building was on fire in downtown Manhattan. The call said people were trapped above the fire on level four and residents were hanging out on balconies"

So simply set up the scene as you would if you were on the phone to a friend telling them what happened.

"When we got there eleven minutes after the call..." and then go on with the story in the basic order that it happened.

So let's review what's happen so far in building the body of the story.

Johnny Robinson has taken to the stage after being introduced. (More on introductions later and why it is so important to get a good one!)

He has started with the OPEN. Simply said hello and said what he will talk about.

Then he's moved on, to the BODY of the story - setting the scene first and then 'coloring in' the details and he continues to the end of the story,

Then it's time for the CLOSE.

Tell your story in your own sweet way. If it helps you, stick to a chronological order, or the sequence in which it happened.

Johnny may have gone on and said...

"The first thing we did was make sure all the people were out of the building. This is pretty tough sometimes at multi-story buildings."

He continues with the story about how a number of residents were rescued from their balconies.

"The long ladder reached most of them quickly.

By then we had accounted for most of the residents and were starting to win the battle against the flames."

Johnny begins to get emotional when relating the part of the story when there were several people they could not get to.

"We thought all of them were safe. Suddenly there were screams from the corner balcony. A woman and her child were trapped by the advancing flames and were overcome by the billowing smoke"

At this stage the audience is completely silent and Johnny explains what happened next.

Johnny stops to compose himself.

"Being a fireman is a rewarding job but sometimes there is just nothing you can do when a victim is in trouble"

The audience gasps audibly as if they know what is coming.

Want to know what happens next as Johnny gets to the meatiest part of the story?

Of course you do.

Let's just say the story had a dramatic but happy ending

Can you see how a story builds during the body and he audience is gripped, hanging on your every word?

Now your story may or may not have that type of appeal, however can you see how this works?

Please let go of any feelings on what you think YOUR audience may in fact think of your speech.

Your genuine feelings will shine through no matter how much experience you have or don't have. **Just being yourself** when you are telling a story is one of the keys to being a proficient or even great speaker.

Be yourself ...be yourself ...be yourself. This point cannot be driven home any harder.

Having guided literally thousands of people to speak and appear 'on-camera' for television and corporate video presentations, this is the key point that gets hammered home.

People like you for who you are,

not what you are trying to be or

even worse, PRETENDING to be.

To be able to allow your 'real' self to come out, you really need to RELAX. If relaxing under 'pressure' (i.e. in front of an audience) is difficult for you, try to imagine that everyone in the room is your friend. Phew - I can relax now.

And if you screw up in any way, they will love you for it!

Here's a quick little story from my early days presenting - it might make you feel better!

While giving a presentation to a group of business people, I was using a white board - you know those ones on wheels you can flip over? During the speak, the wheels moved closer and closer to edge of the stage. It must have been distracting for the audience because every time it got close, I simply rolled it back again. However, I got so 'into' the speak at one point, I failed to notice one of these movements! The board edged closer and

closer, finally it toppled over the edge and crashed onto the floor. OMG!

You know what the audience did as I was literally freaking out inside?

They roared laughing and clapped like crazy! Thankfully a couple of kind souls hoisted the board back on stage. I took a theatrical bow and got on with it. I didn't know what else to do!

A big lesson - everyone screws up.

Most audiences will be kind to you.

So to wrap up –
once again it's a simple
three step dance!

The OPEN is to simply introduce yourself and what you will be speaking about.

The BODY is the main part. This is where your story unfolds.

The CLOSE is how you end 'cleanly' and definitely.

With each speech you plan, use this formula and break it down into the three parts.

You will find it much easier to stay on track and deliver a heartfelt and genuinely entertaining and engaging 'speak'.

At this point you may be thinking "OK I get how you OPEN… just basically say hello and tell the good people in the audience what I'm going to be talking about".

That's right.

"Then I tell my story like I would be telling a friend what happened ... and finally I CLOSE, which is simply thanking the audience, saying I hope you enjoyed it and then accepting the applause."

Sounds easy doesn't it? It is.

At the very least you now know how to approach speaking in public.

You are three from three.

But wait there's more!

We've gone through the 'mechanical' part of how you put the speech together, the natural order it goes in and I hope you are 'getting it'.

Understanding 'WHAT' to do is half the battle and should give your confidence levels a genuine boost.

The next part solves what is the ultimate BIGGIE for most people ... "WHAT WILL I TALK ABOUT?"

Chapter 17: The How

Too often speakers might have a good speech in terms of content but find themselves failing miserably in the delivering.

Evaluate you delivery skills--your weaknesses and strengths. What have people told you? What have you told yourself? Where does the truth lie? This is where self evaluation tests such as those involving self-esteem and personality assessments can play a role. What is your self-esteem like when it comes to public speaking? Your answer to this question could help determine the level of self-confidence you bring to the podium and convey to your audience. Remember self-esteem is not set in stone. So it would be a good idea to consider your speech as a challenge that would help to build higher self-esteem in that area.

Are you an introvert or an extrovert, or a mixture of both? You might use such a question as a guide to assess how comfortable you feel in front of an audience. Being comfortable is important in establishing eye contact with your audience. Many texts have been written about the importance of eye contact as a key element in engaging or connecting with your audience. I'll talk more about this technique in my Anxiety chapter, but I'll mention here that it's something that you need to accept as necessary, so you need to make an effort to do it and in the course of time it should come more naturally.

That dwindling Attention Span….

There's a lot of discussion out there bemoaning the fact (according to a variety of studies) that our attention span is on a rapid decline. Add new technology to the mix and you realize that keeping audience attention and interest is becoming more of an uphill battle. Do I have the interest of the audience from the beginning of my speech? Maybe I can show a brief video (cued before speech), tell a little story or give some astounding statistics to get their attention. I might include some visuals and some charts in the course of the speech, to keep audience interest going, making sure that my visuals are appropriate, easily understood, and well integrated into my speech.

When it comes to speech content, you don't want to be overwhelming your audience with too much information or underwhelming them with a lack of substance. Moreover, in keeping audience interest, variation in tone and volume is very important (See Sleepy language).

Aqua-colored waves rippling gently onto a white-sanded tropical beach ….

What about fluency? Am I using words or phrases as transitions or bridges from one point to the next? When rehearsing your speech, try imagining a gorgeous day at the beach—blue sky, sun glinting on greenish water. Listen to your transitions. Are they as smooth as the waves undulating around you? Try not to replace this ocean view with one of a grey and gloomy day where the waves are choppy and being tossed around at will by wind and pouring rain. This new picture tells a story of a disjointed and scattered speech. It is saying that your fluency needs some serious work.

If you have the habit of using headings or categories before getting into your points, make sure you transition well into these, otherwise, you'll sound like a reader of notes rather than a speaker of note.

The impression you give….

First impression and lasting impression are created from how you begin and how you end your speech. Stumbling over words and not making eye contact might give a first impression of ineptitude, and your audience will probably empathize—they know how it is. But they expect you to improve as you go along. And you can improve. You have the time. It's still early days yet. So don't be discouraged at this point. Put it behind you and move on.

I should mention though, especially to students, that when you stumble, do try to avoid making unintelligible garbled sounds like "Bleh" and "Brrlll" and the like, sometimes accompanied by (**Good Grief**) a sticking out of the tongue. Evidently, such sounds are attempts to communicate to your audience that "I messed up" or "my bad," and your audience will often, understandably, agree with you. After all it **is** public speaking. But making these sounds only further amplifies your mistakes by drawing negative attention to yourself. Too many of those bursts of what I refer to as **gibblygab,** and you might set off your front-row people into thinking of **barf** bags or running for cover. So keep your negative comments—spoken and unspoken—to yourself, and in my chapter on Anxiety, I'll tell you what to do with them.

Lasting impression depends on your overall performance but it also covers how you end your speech. Endings must be smooth, not rough and abrupt. Briefly summarize your key points and leave the audience with something to chew on. Never say "that's it" "that's about it, folks" or "that's my speech." Your audience needs closure and not to be left confused wondering, "Is she done?" "Could have fooled me!"

Think of the overall impression you'd like to give to and leave with your audience. Then you need to ask yourself these questions before your speech: What will my body language be like? What will my nonverbals be saying? Check yourself during the speech. "Am I slouching and slumping? Frowning and scowling?" If you are guilty of some or all of the above, you are telling your audience without words, "I don't want to be here." Your audience members are probably thinking, "Me too." For appearance's sake....

Tied in with impression is the image you'd want to present to your audience. For instance, how am I dressed? Is my attire suitable for the occasion? Am I dressed down instead of being dressed up or vice versa? What about my audience? How do they expect me to dress? Some of these questions would already have been answered in your **Who** step.

What are my natty jeans, old faded T-shirt the-cat-dragged-through-a-fence, saying in a formal situation? What about all the big lettering splashed across my chest? Cool, isn't it? Probably—but not for this occasion. It is a distraction you could do without.

Is my hair neat? Head gear such as caps and bandanas are too trendy and casual for such a setting. Chewing gum is a **no no.** Apart from being unprofessional, it doesn't facilitate clear speaking. In other words, it encourages garbled language. It's hard to believe but I have actually encountered a few speakers who donned eye gear (dark-tinted glasses), to "hide" behind. Don't be impressed. Besides giving the impression of being hung over, you are seriously ruining your chances of success by eliminating eye contact, which as you know by now, is a key element in connecting with your audience.

I hope you never have to wonder why the speaker who introduced you, stepped back--somewhat abruptly. Could this unexpected action have anything to do with, maybe--body odor (BO)? Running errands before going to give a speech is definitely not a good idea. Waiting to shower until later in the day is even worse. And did you chomp through a Tuna sandwich in a hurry without reaching for the mouthwash? How about making some time to floss as well. Some of you might be familiar with the spinach in the teeth scenario where your audience is looking at your face in fascination for the wrong reasons. Don't let that happen to you. Likewise don't drench yourself with cologne or perfume. "Overpowering" should refer to a great speech, not describe what perfume or cologne you are wearing.

Podiums can be empowering....

Speakers have a choice of using podiums or remaining free standing. It's up to the setting and the organizers. One big advantage about podiums is that they bring formality to an event and help to stabilize a speaker's movements while providing a focal point in the room. As a result, they can be quite empowering.

When using a podium, do not hold unto any part of it for dear life. Do not hide behind it or hunch over it or lean on it. Rest both hands slightly on its edges. Check that your hands are not distracting the audience. Do not fiddle with your clothes, hair, earrings and other accessories.

If you are not using a podium, free standing can work very well if you take advantage of the freedom to make more eye contact with your audience and move with ease and deliberation.

But watch for those hands again. On some occasions you might opt to hold a microphone in one hand or occasionally put a hand in a trouser pocket to convey confidence. Very effective with well-seamed trousers, I might add. But generally, the too casual and restrictive hands-in-pockets approach is not encouraged. Keep your hands at your side when not gesturing. Try clasping your hands very loosely in front of you (preferably at waist level). As the podium is not there as a stabilizer, watch for restless moving around. Moreover, stay within the designated speaking space at the front of the room. Don't walk up and down the aisle. You are not doing a workshop where your movements can be more flexible.

Notes can be tricky….

Handling your notes should not be an activity that raises your stress. Increase your font size so that you can see your words easily without having to bend down and squint. If your speech is written out on sheets of paper, increase spaces between points. Doing so helps you to keep your place and avoid awkward pauses or dead air while you are trying to find your spot.

Do not staple your sheets together. It's awkward to maneuver a bulk of material. Instead, make sure your papers are clearly numbered and loose so that you can easily slide each sheet to the side after use.

If you are using visuals remember that you are the focal point; not the screen. Visuals are there to support what you are saying and not to take over the show. You might not want to be the star of this particular show because of speech anxiety but you are. The aids have to be happy with their supporting roles.

The time that you spend….

How much time you have to speak would also dictate how you say it. Prepare your speech with the time in mind; edit your speech with the time in mind; rehearse you speech with the time in mind. Use your time well. Pace yourself so that you don't have to rush through the latter part of your speech after spending too much time on the first part. Do not eat into the time allotted for another speaker. It's like taking food from another person's plate without their permission.

Very bad form.

Chapter 18: Peak Performance Tips

At the risk of repeating myself and stating the obvious, let me again reiterate – no matter what you do, you will always be physiologically aroused prior to and during any speech or presentation. There is an often used saying that if you don't feel at least a **little** nervous before a speech, you must be dead. No one wants or expects a comatose zombie to be making the speech so your goal should never be to eliminate all arousal. Controlled arousal is good. It motivates you to prepare. It gives your speech liveliness and passion.

Acknowledging this, here are some tips to ensure you execute the best possible presentation, with the least possible anxiety –

Take time for introspection

A lot of people I talk to on this topic report having a long-term fear of public speaking, yet very few are entirely certain as to **why** they are fearful. Most people can get as far as **"I am afraid I will embarrass myself"**, however when you go one level deeper – Why are you afraid of embarrassing yourself? – these same people are usually stumped, or say **"being embarrassed feels bad"**.

Taking some time to really dig deep into your automatic, unconscious motivations can be incredibly helpful in terms of guiding how you respond. In particular, what usually happens is that you will trace things back to an illogical assumption like

"Everyone will think I am mentally unstable, so my career will be over"

"Everyone will think that I am not qualified to talk on this subject"

"I will get fired for messing this up"

In my experience, if you are able to have enough introspective clarity, invariably our fears regarding public speaking are a function of unconscious survival instincts.

For example, for the people whose fear is tracked back to their career and ultimately, money, are manifesting ancient drives to have sufficient resources to survive. In this sense, your fear of public speaking has the caveman equivalent where you are afraid you won't be able to source enough food for your tribe or family. The other major driver is around social implications. By sheer coincidence, yesterday I was working on the new edition of Your Plastic Brain and covered this exact topic. As I mention in the book, so many of our modern day motivations and fears can be traced back to very basic survival instincts. In fact, even survival instincts can be questioned if you are feeling sufficiently metaphysical or philosophical. Why do you want to survive? In the time before humans evolved, the survival instinct had one purpose only – to keep you alive long enough for you to pass on your genes. However with our modern prefrontal cortex, we wish to survive for a range of reasons. So you may be wondering how embarrassment and survival are linked in our subconscious. If we go back millions of years ago, being socially ostracized could mean expulsion from the tribe. And being alone during that period would have been exceedingly dangerous, with limited prospects for survival, or more importantly, mating – to pass on your genes.

So as ridiculous as it sounds, our brains often associate looking nervous or flubbing your lines during a presentation, with a risk to our survival. Hence why you experience such an intense fight or flight reaction. Our amygdala is the ultimate irrational thinker. Clearly by activating your fight or flight response, your amygdala is telling you to "get the hell out of here, now!" However, for you, which would be more embarrassing – appearing nervous or fleeing the room? If only it were easier to ignore our amygdala's awful advice!

Here are some tips and tricks on different approaches and some of the questions you need to address –

Considering that embarrassment causes you no physical harm, does not impair your career ambitions and won't change your friendships, why is the fear of embarrassment such a powerful force?

Imagine a hypothetical scenario where, instead of 30 adult professionals, you are presenting to 30 toddlers or 30 teenagers. Does it still fill you with the same fear? If not, why not?

Test your assumptions. Imagine you were simply a computer and make an unemotional assessment of whether your assumptions are correct or not. By shining a light on these assumptions, if you are able to demonstrate in your own mind that they are faulty, gradually your amygdala starts to believe it also

Each time you answer a question in your mind, keep asking questions until you get close to the nucleus of your fears. For example –

Why am I afraid of public speaking? I don't want to look foolish when I get nervous and start messing up my presentation.

Why? Whenever the audience thinks of me again, all they will remember was that loser who turned into a blabbering fool. My reputation will be shot.

Have you ever heard of someone's reputation being ruined by looking nervous during a presentation? **Well, no...but...**

Why is your reputation important to you? If I get a bad reputation as mentally fragile, no one will hire me again.

Why does the idea of not getting hired scare you? Because I won't have enough money to pay for things like food or housing.

And so on…

When you discover an irrational assumption, work to replace it with a true assumption, like –

What seems to me like a disaster, most people in the room probably never even noticed.

Almost everyone looks at least a little nervous during presentations – it's expected. If you look nervous or make some mistakes, the audience is unlikely to think twice about it.

Even if you have a literal melt-down (which is exceedingly unlikely, despite what your amygdala might be telling you), the audience will mostly empathise with you ("We've all been there"). No-one will think you are incompetent/fragile (or whatever else putdown you apply to yourself) just because you had a presentation which didn't go as well as you'd hoped

Know your subject

If you don't know your subject inside out, you will lack confidence and it will show. This is also one of the greatest potential sources of anxiety or panic, because you may either be worried subconsciously that you are a fraud or you are worried that you will become derailed during the speech due to a lack of understanding. If you make sure you are **the** authority on the subject you are talking about, your confidence will show.

Chapter 19: Pre-Preparation

How many seminars have you gone to and paid good money to participate in, only to find the speaker reading from cards, or reading from an overhead presentation? And let us not forget the "and, ums, ah's".

I attended a seminar awhile back and it was so bad that I found myself counting how many "and's and um's" were being stated. I really cannot remember what the subject was. I found myself viewing the seminar participants sleeping, writing, daydreaming and so on. Have you ever been to one of those? There are really only two major causes for this type of poor performance.

1. Just there to get paid

This is the most disgusting reason of all. If your public speaking career is solely based on the monetary return and not 100% passionate about your speaking career, GET OUT! People pay good money for seminars and expect to hear a good presenter with good skills and information. Nuf said!

2. Bad preparation

Pre-preparation is critical to delivering a good presentation. In public speaking the prepreparation, or lack of, will be quickly noticed by your audience.

We are going to address pre-seminar preparation.

So, now you have the subject matter for your next seminar. You know the venue and the time allotted for your presentation. What else do you need to know?

Elements of Pre Prep

You should start pre-preparation two weeks in advance for a new speech and a week for a presentation you have given before. You will find that you will deliver the same presentation several times in your public speaking career. It will become almost second nature. **Don't get caught in the complacency trap here!** As your presentations on the same subject are delivered multiple times they become aged. So the presentation you present now could very well be outdated tomorrow. With the speed of technology and the "information highway" always in a state of flux, you can become outdated almost over night. Stay current with your subject. Employ the new technologies available to stay current with your audience.

Know your audience

This is a critical element of your success as a public speaker. You must know your audience before you can really get into the pre

 preparation. Know their age group, gender, ethnicity, education, income level, etc. You may ask yourself, "Why do I need to know all this information?"

The more your presentation is geared towards a specific audience, the more impact and success you will have in its delivery and the less chance of a blunder. Example: There was a speech given by a government official where a question was raised on how the presenter thought about a specific person. His response was… Me personally, I felt the response was well stated. Others found it offensive with regard to "he is articulate" and it was taken as a racial insult. In this new, politically correct (PC), world, one must be careful with one's words. **People today have become a lot more sensitive and personally I feel way over sensitive about spoken words. I think to the extreme. In fact, it's ridiculous!** Actually, "free speech" is being attacked everyday. This is a freedom we have and should not be taken lightly. Enough of the politics, but I thought it should be stated. Anyway, as you can see, understanding your audience is crucial. Not spending time in this very important step of your pre-preparation could adversely affect your presentation.

To find out information on your audience, contact the event planner. They would have a good idea of your audience's makeup. If you're not satisfied with the results of that investigation, seek out more. The time dedicated to finding the makeup of your audience is invaluable as you will soon find out in the next chapter. Once you are satisfied with the results of this investigation you can make adjustments to your presentation and delivery style, as applicable.

Here is a tid-bit that may help in understanding your audience. There is a big difference between an all female audience and an all male audience. All female audiences tend to laugh more easily and louder than all male audiences. All-male audiences are the toughest because ego gets in the way of laughter. They look around to see if anyone else is laughing before they laugh, and they won't laugh as loud because they think they will look less powerful and really don't want to draw attention to them.

One of the most challenging audiences is a group of executives from the same company where the "Top-Dog" is in attendance, like the President or CEO. This is what happens more often than not. You say something funny, the audience will start to laugh, but they will kind of hold off as they check to see if the "Top-Dog" is laughing. If he or she is laughing, then they go ahead and laugh. **To me this is weak! I really don't care who is in attendance. If something is funny, I will laugh.**

Audiences that are more than 50 percent female are good because the presence of females provides a good buffer and makes it okay for the men to laugh, since so many other people are laughing. **It's a macho thing!**

Speech Preparation - Okay, you have your subject, now what? Organizing your speech is an important skill to learn. Good organization is often the key to understanding. The audience is more likely to understand your message if it is well-organized and delivered. Write out your speech. Writing for public speaking isn't so different from other types of writing. You want to hold your audience's attention, communicate your ideas in a logical manner and use reliable evidence to support your point.

When you write a speech, understand your audience is made up of listeners. They have only one chance to comprehend what you're presenting. Your speech must be well-organized with a solid introduction, body and conclusion. Your delivery must be easily understood, and must fit the audience. Again with the audience!

Practice, Practice, Practice! - In my eyes this is the most important part of public

speaking! You will be in front of this audience only once, you blow it here and you're all done. I'm not joking!

If this is a new subject, you need to start practicing this presentation one week before show time! Your reputation is riding on every presentation you present, regardless of the public speaking venue. Ask a friend over to help. It may cost you a dinner or beer, but, present it and ask for honest feedback. I would strongly suggest investing in a video camera for yourself. Record your presentation at home. That's to include the suit and tie... "the whole nine." Now play it back! You are your worst critic. Takes notes of what you see and hear everything from voice inflection, to delivery style. How did you do addressing the subject? Have a couple of friends watch the video and give their reactions. The video camera is a great tool for you to pick up on the little things.

It is not a good practice to read off cue cards or from a Power Point presentation.

Your audience can read the onscreen presentation. It does not hurt to glance up if you lose your place. If you practiced this presentation enough, you shouldn't have to.

Equipment Requirements - Understand your venue. Seating capacity, number of expected participants, size of room and acoustics play a huge roll on your planned delivery. Find out about existing sound equipment, projectors, screens and lighting.

 Once you have gathered all this information you can start your pre-prep for equipment needed like wireless microphone systems and adaptability to existing sound equipment, USB presentation projectors, laptops, extra batteries, extra bulbs, USB flash drive (backup for your presentation), and screens. The night before you are scheduled to depart, load all your required equipment into your car or a staging area. Why the night before? Well we all know the day of travel is hectic. You might wake up late and have to rush and could easily forget something important for your presentation. By preloading or pre staging all is ready and you can focus on the upcoming event without any anxiety.

You will, as your speaking career grows, start picking your audiences. Yes, I did say pick your audiences. Most rated speakers don't accept every offer to speak even if they are available, and the money is right. They pick their events to put themselves in front of audiences whose profile indicates the best chance of success.

Yes, there are some of you that may not have this luxury because you're speaking as part of your job. When you are a beginning public speaker it is important for you to experience different types of audiences to gain the experience. As you ascend the public speaking ladder you will know the value of picking your audience. Just say no when the audience is not a fit.

There is nothing worst than getting to your public speaking venue and you don't have the correct equipment for your presentation. Backup, back-up backup! Basically, be prepared for the worst!

Pre-preparation is critical to your public speaking career. Know your audience, write out your speech in a logical manner, practice, practice, practice and then practice some more. Video tape your presentation and review. Understand your venue and have the required equipment there to present your best presentation ever!

Chapter 20: Public Speaking Visualization

Assume your most comfortable position now. You may choose to lie down on the floor, or sit with your legs crossed. Do not fold your arms across your chest; just let them lie on your sides. Make sure your back is flat on the wall or the ground so you won't feel any strain.

As you close your eyes, remember that you are a being of light. You are a person bestowed with many talents. Let this thought linger in your mind for a while, as you concentrate in your breathing. Breathe in and breathe out. In this visualization process, the only great thing is you. You are wonderful. You are connected to the Universe.

Now, relax and fully let go. Let go of your fears of public speaking. Let go of your anxieties and notions that you aren't good enough. Listen to your own breathing, to the beat of your own heart, to the call of your soul. Take a long deep breath and imagine a blue light in your throat. This blue ball of light is just there, hovering in your throat. It is cool in that region, and this light is loosening up whatever tension built up there. This is your throat chakra, and the light is healing you of whatever communication troubles you may have.

In your mind's eye, visualize yourself becoming more and more relaxed now. In the room where you are in, you are attuned with nature. From where you are, flowers bloom. Blue and lavender flowers gently touch your skin. You can feel the flowers near your toes, beneath your back, and beneath your head. Allow the flowerbed to nurture you. They have been called by the blue light from the throat chakra region.

You can now feel the warm breeze floating around you. This is nature responding to you. This is Mother Nature absorbing all the negativity in your body. The blue light in your throat is radiating more brightly now, empowering you and your talents. After this guided imagery exercise, you will feel more empowered, enthusiastic, optimistic, and confident. Let the earth capture your negative thoughts about public speaking. Similarly, allow the blue light to work on their behalf to help you speak, and speak well.

Imagine yourself standing before a crowd and feeling more confident as you stand there. You are facing hundreds of people who want to listen to you. You are facing these people who want to listen to your message. You feel good about this. You feel good and empowered just by seeing these people. You feel good about talking before this crowd.

You have prepared a wonderful speech for them. Picture yourself well-prepared for this task. You know that you can nail this performance. Envision yourself already speaking before the crowd, giving them the introduction to your piece and amazing them at the onset. Imagine that the audience is all ears with you. They are intently watching out for anything you'd say. You feel confident as you look into the faces of these people, knowing that you would be able to articulate your message very well. You are not afraid at all. You believe in yourself.

As you talk, envision the crowd nodding in assent. They see what you mean and believe what you say. They believe in your ability. As such, you will not let them down. As you get to the body of your speech, you become more and more energized, more confident, and more motivated to drive your message across. You are amazed by this power within you. You are amazed because you can articulate your message with ease. You are not stuttering. You are not at a loss for words. Imagine yourself as the best speaker the audience has ever heard.

Picture them laughing at a joke you said. They are looking at you, eager to listen for more. These people want to learn from you. In return, you give them what they wish to know.

Take another deep breath and focus on how you feel at the moment. You feel glorious now. You feel definitely in control of your speech. You have memorized this speech and you know you will not falter. It is easy for you to go on ad lib because you know your topic by heart.

Focus on how your heart beats. In the past, you used to feel nervous when making a great speech. But now, all you feel is tremendous happiness because you are sharing your message to the world. You are proud of what you have achieved. You are proud of what you have become.

Release any tension and remember this vision every time you speak before a crowd. They believe in you, and you must not lose faith in yourself. You are a great speaker. Acknowledge this truth.

Chapter 21: Have A Clear Focus / Message

It is essential to have a very clearly defined focus for your presentation. This is the central message, the key take-away that you want each audience member to 100% internalize when they leave the room. It is important both that you discover what your focus is, and that you articulate it well for the audience.

A clear focus to your presentation is important because:

It ensures excellent communication with the audience. If what you are talking about seems grey and feels intellectually loose/unclear around the edges, it will be harder to explain it and thus harder for others to understand it.

When you create and communicate that clear focus, you can develop more complex ideas by working outward from that core. Only through clear expression of something definite can you build upward into more complicated ideas. Like building a house, only strong, well-defined bricks can be built upon. Ensure that the ideas that follow have a clear focus, themselves.

It will be a lot easier for you to both create the presentation and to give it. There will be a lot less "What should I talk about next?" and "Is this really what I want to say now?" because the whole presentation will have a clear focus from which all the related information will organically proceed.

To determine the focus of your presentation, you will need to refine your ideas into shorter summary sentences. Start by simply getting all of your ideas down on paper. Then, cut down your sentences and continually re-word phrases into more concise and accurate expressions. Ideally, you should be able to get it down to a sentence. The 140 characters that Twitter allows makes a very specific limit, and if you manage to get your focus to the length of a tweet, you can also then spread your message on social media to promote your presentation.

To clearly articulate the focus of your presentation, it is easiest to say it right off the bat and/or have it projected behind you. Consider returning to this core message throughout your presentation as well as leaving it onscreen at the end. Of course, including it on handouts, social media updates, posters, etc. will all help make your focus 100% clear. These steps help you communicate the focus perfectly; however, having a clear focus won't always make the best presentation.

Some kind of "slow reveal" throughout your presentation can be a better way to keep your audience's attention and pique their curiosity. Also, consider using pre-presentation marketing that perhaps focuses more on a sales-pitch message, **e.g**., posters that focus on benefits of the presentation. That strategy will often be more effective to get people through the door than perhaps expressing explicitly the message of your presentation.

Through understanding the objective of your presentation, you can better decide how rigorously you want to communicate its core focus. It will, however, always be helpful to ascertain the focus for you to work on in the presentation, and to communicate it 100% at some point in your presentation—even if you only do so at the end.

Make Great Eye Contact

Making eye contact probably isn't a new idea to you. Good eye contact is advisable both when talking to new people and socializing at work. To a similar, and if anything, greater extent, making great eye contact is an important part of giving a great presentation.

Many studies have discovered that people who make higher levels of eye contact are considered to be:

Trustworthy and more honest. This translates to people believing what you have to say in your presentation.

Confident and powerful. If your audience sees that you believe in your message, they will be much more inclined to believe in it, as well.

Attractive and likeable. This one is obvious. If your audience likes you, they're going to like the presentation.

And so great eye contact really is essential to giving a great presentation. The above points should have sold you on the idea, but if they haven't, think of it this way – it is the easiest, fastest "fix" to improve your presentation. It takes time to tweak your ideas, your slides, and how you tell a story. But to simply look the audience in the eyes more – that adjustment can be instant.

Now, I hear some of you say "Yes, it doesn't take any time to start doing it, but it's kinda scary meeting that much eye contact when public speaking!" And the cure to this concern is simple: don't quite look people in the eye. Instead, look at their foreheads, or at another point so close that it will only **seem** as if you are looking them in the eye. This will feel less stressful than full-on eye contact.

It can also be helpful to make more eye contact with audience members that you aren't in any way intimidated by. Don't try to stare down the business manager in the front row if he/she intimidates you. The same goes for the guy/girl you think is kind of cute in the second row. Ignore them, and pick whoever looks least intimidating to you; give these unintimidating people the lion's share of your eye contact.

If there is a large room of people, it can be difficult to know with whom you should begin to make eye contact and how to share it out through the room. There is no definite rule, except that you need to share your eye contact relatively evenly with all areas in the room. Every "section" of the audience needs to be engaged regularly by your strong, confident eye contact. The simplest way to distribute eye contact is to divide the audience into three sections: left, centre, and right. Then pick someone roughly in the middle of each section, and return to these three people periodically.

Making eye contact needs to feel natural and organic to the audience – don't give people a stare that makes them fear for their lives. Imagine you are making eye contact with an old friend.

When getting feedback from friends/colleagues in your practice presentations, work to refine the amount of eye contact you make. Ask whether you are giving enough eye contact, and whether it feels like you're creating the right kind of "vibe."

Keep it Short and Break it Up into Sections
Many people who are still learning how to give a great presentation make the mistake of thinking that more content equals a better presentation. This mistake is common among people on the cusp of

delivering something great; indeed, these people may have put in a lot of work to make a presentation they believe is awesome. But they tragically overstep the mark and mistakenly trade more content for clarity, communication, and a compelling overall presentation.

Keeping things brief helps for a variety of reasons. Below are a few:

Remember that time is precious, and your presentation is not only taking up one or two people's time, but a whole group's. It will come across as disrespectful and aggravating if you fail to stay on-point. You can even say "I want to respect your time, so I'm going to keep this focused, and no longer than it needs be." Making a statement like this will remind you to stay on point, and it will put everyone at ease.

Brief presentations tend to be the ones with the clearest focus. As soon as you start elaborating, digressing, or giving extra content, you risk move further away from the key message. Imagine that the audience has their arms open, and you are giving them things to carry out. By delivering excessive content, you give them more than they can carry, and they end up dropping items and possibly leaving with nothing at all. Give the audience the most important and briefest of ideas so that they can easily carry away those key points.

It's obviously easier to hold people's attention for shorter periods of time. Keeping your presentation brief will help keep everyone on board and prevent distractions of focus. Consider this tip especially if your presentation is approaching an hour in length. At some point, people are going to need to take a bathroom break, check phones, etc., and then the attention of the group will begin to drop off rapidly.

As well as keeping your presentation brief overall, it is helpful to break your presentation up into clearly defined sections. Clear sections help the audience both understand and remember what you have to say because you are giving them clearly defined and digestible chunks. It's like cutting up a big piece of food for someone to eat, instead of just handing them the whole thing and blithely expecting them to deal with it.

Breaking up your presentation will also allow small breaks for yourself and everyone in the room, even if only a few seconds for everyone to compose themselves and recharge. If your presentation is long (30+ minutes), then break it up into smaller, brief ones. Let people leave the room if they have been sitting for a long time, or work activities into the breaks so that people can physically learn about the message you have been sharing with them.

Smile, Be Positive, and Upbeat

No one wants to be presented to by someone who is unhappy, or afraid of smiling. Liberally dose your presentation with plenty of sincere and relaxed smiles.

Better still, get yourself into a genuinely positive, happy mode, and bring that spirit into your presentation.

Smiling and bringing upbeat, happy energy will help because the audience will associate your presentation with positive emotions; in turn, they will want to believe in it and take action on the core message. Also, you'll enjoy it more – presentations can be enjoyable, I promise you!

Below are some ideas on how to bring upbeat, positive energy to your presentation by getting yourself pumped up and feeling good.

Get some exercise in beforehand. Go for a hard bike ride, a long run, or lift some weights. Get the blood pumping around your body and enjoy those natural endorphins. You will feel calmer, happier, and more focused. There really is no reason not to.

Listen to your favourite music really loudly before you begin, and dance around shamelessly (in private).

Go out for an amazing night/meal with your closest friends the night before. That positive energy will spill over into the following day. Don't turn up hungover or tired, though.

Watch an episode of your favourite comedy show earlier in the day. Let yourself laugh, and enjoy every second of it. Better still, watch it with some friends, and laugh together.

Eat something that is light and delicious. You don't want to be digesting a heavy meal beforehand. A roast dinner and dessert an hour before your presentation is sure to sabotage you by causing only feelings of lethargy and poor focus. Opt instead for a tuna salad or something similar.

As well as getting yourself into a great state, why not get the whole room pumped up and feeling good? Tony Robbins is a master of high-energy presentations, so watch him on YouTube if you want to see how it is done right.

Below are some ideas on how you can do something similar:

Be aware of the mood in the room. Are people disinterested, interested, happy? Try to guide them emotionally, as well as through the intellectual ideas you are discussing.

Include jokes and light ideas to balance out the more serious material you are covering.

Include fun activities that get the audience moving around. Have them high-five each other after they complete a task you have given them. Get their blood pumping, and get them socializing with one another. They'll feel more relaxed, more upbeat, and this will all lead to a better experience for them.

Chapter 22: Realism Not Perfection

Stop aiming for perfection.

I am not saying this to make you unmotivated. On the contrary, I want you to realize that you are good enough—you just refuse to see it because you keep thinking that you're supposed to be perfect.

This is why it is important to be realistic—and stop being such an extremist in your head. Read on, and you'll be able to understand this better.

The Fantasy Land

Every anxious person has a fantasy land in their heads. And no, this fantasy land doesn't have any faeries or dwarves in it. It has such unrealistic expectations that could really drive everyone insane.

More often than not, people think of speeches as things that could make or break them. But, instead of focusing on the "make" part, they focus on the "break" of the equation. They feel that their speech would only be successful if all parts of it have gone right.

For example:

A speech is only successful once every single person in the room has laughed—otherwise, it means they don't understand what you have said.

Every single person in the room has to love your presentation.

Your diction should be flawless.

You cannot use even one single filler.

If you make a mistake, it means you are a failure.

Cut the crap! No one is perfect and you do not have to be that **hard** on yourself. It doesn't help. It never will.

A speech doesn't have to define you as a person. Sure, you want it to be perfect—but it doesn't mean that everything will go right. After all, you cannot please everybody, and thinking that you can will only drive you nuts. The important thing is to feel that even just a single part of that room is able to understand you.

Even the best speakers cannot please everyone—and there is no problem with that.

The Reality Check Scale

"I'm going to die while making the speech!"

"No one is going to like this!"

Here you go with your negative way of thinking again.

People are fond of catastrophes. They turn rains into storms, summers into droughts, etc. Sometimes, when you make expressions like **"I'm going to die while making the speech!"** you think that it's true—even if there's really no truth to it.

But ask yourself: Are you really going to die during a speech? Probably not.

Sometimes, you have to get back down to earth and realize that hey, just because you're fond of catastrophes in your head does not mean they will come true. You are always better than you think you are. Stop making room for absolutes.

Again: you are not perfect—and no one else is, so what's the problem? You are not going to die. Relax.

Bring it on

Have you seen the movie **Bring it on**? Well, one thing about the **Toros** (the cheerleaders in the said movie) is that they're always ready.

You know why?

It's because they went through every single aspect of the program and have prepared for it. It doesn't guarantee perfection, sure, but at least, it would help you know what to expect, and it would also help you get started on your speech in the best possible manner.

Here are some of the things you should keep in mind:

When exactly will you deliver the speech, and where?

Where will you be waiting before you get onstage?

Do you know how big the stage is?

Who constitutes your target audience?

Have you already made an outline? If not, make one now.

Have you actually researched for your speech?

Are you preparing for a Q and A session?

If yes, what questions will you be asking? And, are you prepared to answer the audience's questions, too?

Do you have any props?

Are props important for your speech?

What if there is another speaker invited?

What are you going to wear?

Is the sound system okay? Have you tested it?

How will you get to the venue?

How long will your speech be?

What is the seating plan in the venue?

You see, it's always best to be prepared. This way, even if you cannot attain perfection, you still wouldn't fail your audience—and yourself!

Chapter 23: Getting Your Message Across

I bet you have had times whenever you have walked into a shop and felt instantly welcome. I'm additionally pretty sure that you've had occasions where you've felt just the opposite. What was the difference? What happened in the place that created that welcome feeling within you?

Perhaps the assistant observed you entering and offered you a smile and stated hello. They are telling you that you are welcome in their space both bodily and psychologically. Compare this with a

shop where you were totally ignored until you went to pay for something. What message are you getting there? What's rapport?
Rapport is the art of being 'in tune' with the people around you. Good rapport will allow you to let others know that you are interested in them, that you care about what they have to say and are keen to comprehend them. It sends them a message that there is common ground and creates a sense of consideration, respect and trust.
Good rapport lies at the heart of your efficient communication. It allows you to get people's focus and for them to take onboard what you have to say. Good rapport comes from body gestures and how you say things through the tonality and rhythm of your voice. Together, body gestures and how you say your words make up 93% of your communication. What you say is only 7%! Obviously, when interacting with others

our communication could be non-verbal using just our body gestures. How are you communicating right now? I'm sure that you have experienced a circumstance where within a group of people one person makes a suggestion and you just know that others don't agree - even if they stay silent. What tells you that they don't agree and feel comfy with the suggestion? Those of you who are in agreement will most likely be sharing the same body gestures; they might be more animated in the discussion, and as such will be actively buying in to the idea. Those that disagree could do so without having to say or do a thing. All they need to do is withdraw their rapport in quite a few way; perhaps though pulling back in their seat, crossing their arms, closing their book or leaving the room. Perhaps, through all those things if they truly desired to make a point! So, assuming that we have a number of words to say, how could we maximise our tonality and body gestures to ensue that we have good rapport when saying them?

How to get into rapport with people. Matching and mirroring are the two primary ways to establish rapport. People which are in rapport have a particular rhythm to their voice and body movements.

Voice Tonality and Rhythm. This is 38% of your communication. The tone of your voice and the pace that you talk affects the message that you are attempting to portray. People use different tones and speeds when talking. Do your greatest to adjust your voice to come closer to their way of talking. Try it your self - say something cheerful in a sad voice and see how it comes across, then switch it around and say something sad in an upbeat voice. What message are you receiving in each case? What about when somebody is speaking with you and you are diverted by something else, perhaps something you see? Does your voice reply in an interested manner, and does your body gestures bear this out?

Body gestures. How you hold and use your body makes up 55% of your communication. Use your body to match people's body movements. There will be a specified pattern and rhythm to their movements that you could copy. It's wise to pay focus to this even though you have good intentions for doing otherwise. You could effortlessly be misinterpreted.

How about if that shop assistant smiles and says hello but without looking at you -

does that feel the same? Perhaps she was preparing next week's stock. What if two assistants are chatting whilst you are in their shop even while politely serving you? Does the rapport exist between them or between you and them?

What if in a work environment you ask someone to do something for you and they agree quite well but you could see them tense up or see their body sink slightly lower in their chair? Are they truly joyful to do this for you or are speech and body telling different stories?
All together now!
The next time you communicate think about rapport a bit. Is it good or not? What makes it good? How could you use your body gestures and voice to improve rapport?
And stick with it. It could seem odd at times while you practice but when it becomes second nature you'll turn into a

more   natural   communicator.

Conclusion

Let me get you started the easy way. You need feedback from a friendly audience. This might be friends, colleagues, or maybe even other professionals through an organization such as Toastmasters. With your friendly audience, you're now looking for one or two very specific and clear ticks you currently have. Most normal speakers have one or two things they are doing that effectively make it difficult for the audience to hear their message. It might be a total lack of eye contact, or very dense unreadable slides, a rapid pace no one can follow, or a sharp lack of volume making it impossible to hear them.

Have your friendly audience help you identify what that initial big barrier might be for you. Then go to work. Over the next six months every time you speak in a formal presentation or not, working to become conscious of that behavior and to correctly improve that behavior. You'll be smart to empower a small number of people around you to watch and evaluate that behavior so that you'll know with clarity when you're moving in the right direction. After several months of doing this, when you're confident that the major one or two ticks have been smoothed out considerably, it's then time to put together your friendly audience one more time.

This time they'll hear your message more clearly and see the components of your delivery because you've removed the one or two things that were blinding them from all the rest. Get their feedback and try to integrate it into your speaking for at least a few months. Then go back over the material in this short course one more time. After that, you'll be ready to test out the new you with a more difficult audience. That might be your team, supervisors, vendors, or maybe clients.

Audiences willing and able to give you more critical feedback if you need it. Just remember, it's a marathon not a sprint. So don't try to fix everything at once. Focus on one finite area of improvement at a time. And pretty soon, you'll be becoming a more confident and effective speaker.

www.ingramcontent.com/pod-product-compliance
Lightning Source LLC
Chambersburg PA
CBHW072009070526
44583CB00015B/1399